Perspectives from Literature

Perspectives from Literature

Perspectives from Literature

Editors:
John Willard, Nikhil Deliwala, Donald St. John

Revised: December 2022

Copyright © 2013 by Peter R. Beaven

Printed in the United States of America

All rights reserved. No part of this book may be reproduced or transmitted in any form or by any means, electronic or mechanical, including photocopying, recording, or by any information storage or retrieval system, without permission in writing from the copyright owner.

Beaven and Associates Private Tutors
3 Dundee Park, Suite 202A
Andover, MA 01810

Tel. 978 475-5487
www.beavenandassociates.com

Perspectives from Literature

The word anthology comes to us from the Classical Greek anthos, meaning flowers, and logia, meaning collection. Thanks to the printing press, a collection of stories, essays, chronicles, and observations, when printed out, would be known as an anthology. Perspectives from Literature is an anthology that invites the reader to explore, as an armchair traveler, writings from Homer in Ancient Greece, to those of Jack London in early twentieth century America. Whether venturesome or pragmatic, the student of Perspectives from Literature will sharpen his reading skills answering the questions posed with each selection. He may seek further journeys of the mind in the other books in the series, Perusals, and Perspectives from History.

Contents

World Literature..5
    Genesis – Adam and Eve (circa 1500 BCE)..7
    Homer - The Odyssey (800 BCE)...12
    Miguel Cervantes - Don Quixote (1605)...20
    Grimm brothers – Cinderella (1812)..24
    Anton Chekhov – A Slander (1883) 31

English Literature...35
    Sir Thomas Malory - Morte D'Arthur (1485)..37
    William Shakespeare – Henry V (1599)...40
    Jonathan Swift - Gulliver's Travels (1726) 43
    Charles Dickens – A Tale of Two Cities (1859)...48
    Lewis Carroll - Through the Looking Glass (1871)..52
    H. G. Wells – The Time Machine – XII – (1895)..59
    Rudyard Kipling – How the Leopard Got His Spots (1902)..64
    Kenneth Grahame - Wind in the Willows (1908)..69
    Saki – The Interlopers (1919)..78

American Literature...83
    Edgar Allan Poe - The Tell-Tale Heart (1843)...85
    Herman Melville - Moby Dick (1851)...90
    Harriet Beecher Stowe – Uncle Tom's Cabin (1852)...95
    Joel Chandler Harris - Brer Rabbit and the Tar-Baby (1880).....................................99
    Ambrose Bierce – An Occurrence At Owl Creek Bridge (1891)................................104
    Kate Chopin - The Story of An Hour (1894)..112
    Frank Baum - Wizard of Oz (1900)...115
    Jack London - Call of the Wild (1903)...119
    Upton Sinclair - The Jungle (1906) 123
    O. Henry - Gift of the Magi (1906)...127
    Langston Hughes - Thank You, M'am (1958)...132

Answer Key..137

World Literature

GENESIS – ADAM AND EVE (CIRCA 1500 BCE)

And the LORD God formed man of the dust of the ground, and breathed into his nostrils the breath of life; and man became a living soul.

5 And the LORD God planted a garden eastward in Eden; and there he put the man whom he had formed.

And out of the ground made the LORD God to grow every tree that is pleasant to 10 the sight, and good for food; the tree of life also in the midst of the garden, and the tree of knowledge of good and evil.

And the LORD God took the man, and put him into the garden of Eden to dress it and 15 to keep it.

And the LORD God commanded the man, saying, Of every tree of the garden thou mayest freely eat:

But of the tree of the knowledge of good 20 and evil, thou shalt not eat of it: for in the day that thou eatest thereof thou shalt surely die.

And the LORD God said, It is not good that the man should be alone; I will make him 25 an help meet for him.

And out of the ground the LORD God formed every beast of the field, and every fowl of the air; and brought them unto Adam to see what he would call them: and 30 whatsoever Adam called every living creature, that was the name thereof.

And Adam gave names to all cattle, and to the fowl of the air, and to every beast of the field; but for Adam there was not found an 35 help meet for him.

And the LORD God caused a deep sleep to fall upon Adam, and he slept: and he took one of his ribs, and closed up the flesh instead thereof;

40 And the rib, which the LORD God had taken from man, made he a woman, and brought her unto the man.

And Adam said, This is now bone of my bones, and flesh of my flesh: she shall be

Genesis – Adam and Eve (circa 1500 BCE)

⁴⁵ called Woman, because she was taken out of Man.

Therefore shall a man leave his father and his mother, and shall cleave unto his wife: and they shall be one flesh.

⁵⁰ And they were both naked, the man and his wife, and were not ashamed.

Now the serpent was more subtil than any beast of the field which the LORD God had made. And he said unto the woman, Yea, ⁵⁵ hath God said, Ye shall not eat of every tree of the garden?

And the woman said unto the serpent, We may eat of the fruit of the trees of the garden:

⁶⁰ But of the fruit of the tree which is in the midst of the garden, God hath said, Ye shall not eat of it, neither shall ye touch it, lest ye die.

And the serpent said unto the woman, Ye ⁶⁵ shall not surely die:

For God doth know that in the day ye eat thereof, then your eyes shall be opened, and ye shall be as gods, knowing good and evil.

And when the woman saw that the tree was ⁷⁰ good for food, and that it was pleasant to the eyes, and a tree to be desired to make one wise, she took of the fruit thereof, and did eat, and gave also unto her husband with her; and he did eat.

⁷⁵ And the eyes of them both were opened, and they knew that they were naked; and they sewed fig leaves together, and made themselves aprons.

And they heard the voice of the LORD God ⁸⁰ walking in the garden in the cool of the day: and Adam and his wife hid themselves from the presence of the LORD God amongst the trees of the garden.

And the LORD God called unto Adam, and ⁸⁵ said unto him, Where art thou?

And he said, I heard thy voice in the garden, and I was afraid, because I was naked; and I hid myself.

And he said, Who told thee that thou wast ⁹⁰ naked? Hast thou eaten of the tree, whereof I commanded thee that thou shouldest not eat?

And the man said, The woman whom thou gavest to be with me, she gave me of the ⁹⁵ tree, and I did eat.

And the LORD God said unto the woman, What is this that thou hast done? And the woman said, The serpent beguiled me, and I did eat.

¹⁰⁰ And the LORD God said unto the serpent, Because thou hast done this, thou art cursed above all cattle, and above every beast of the field; upon thy belly shalt thou go, and dust shalt thou eat all the days of thy life:

¹⁰⁵ And I will put enmity between thee and the woman, and between thy seed and her seed; it shall bruise thy head, and thou shalt bruise his heel.

Unto the woman he said, I will greatly mul- ¹¹⁰ tiply thy sorrow and thy conception; in sorrow thou shalt bring forth children; and thy desire shall be to thy husband, and he shall rule over thee.

And unto Adam he said, Because thou hast ¹¹⁵ hearkened unto the voice of thy wife, and hast eaten of the tree, of which I commanded thee, saying, Thou shalt not eat of it: cursed is the ground for thy sake; in sorrow shalt thou eat of it all the days of thy life;

¹²⁰ Thorns also and thistles shall it bring forth to thee; and thou shalt eat the herb of the field;

In the sweat of thy face shalt thou eat bread, till thou return unto the ground; for ¹²⁵ out of it wast thou taken: for dust thou art, and unto dust shalt thou return.

And Adam called his wife's name Eve; because she was the mother of all living.

Genesis – Adam and Eve (circa 1500 BCE)

Unto Adam also and to his wife did the LORD God make coats of skins, and clothed them.

And the LORD God said, Behold, the man is become as one of us, to know good and evil: and now, lest he put forth his hand, and take also of the tree of life, and eat, and live for ever:

Therefore the LORD God sent him forth from the garden of Eden, to till the ground from whence he was taken.

So he drove out the man; and he placed at the east of the garden of Eden Cherubims, and a flaming sword which turned every way, to keep the way of the tree of life.

Genesis – Adam and Eve (circa 1500 BCE)

Exercises

1. Adam is commanded first to:
   A. tend the Garden of Eden
   B. name all the creatures
   C. distinguish between good and evil
   D. find a mate
   E. be wary of the serpent

2. One can infer that Adam names his counterpart "Wo-man" (line 45) to mean:
   A. "woe to man"
   B. helper
   C. gift to man
   D. from man
   E. under man

3. The word "subtil" ['subtle'] (l. 52) pegs the serpent as:
   A. lowly
   B. untrustworthy
   C. evil
   D. inferior
   E. crafty

4. God says the immediate punishment for eating the forbidden fruit will be:
   A. death
   B. sickness
   C. shame
   D. banishment
   E. moral knowledge

5. After eating the forbidden fruit, Adam hides because he:
   A. fears punishment
   B. is unclothed
   C. is sorrowful
   D. feels guilty
   E. is playing with the woman

6. Adam and Eve's knowledge and subsequent covering their bodies suggests their:
   A. cooperativeness
   B. equality
   C. inferiority
   D. morality
   E. need to deceive

7. The major punishment God metes out to the pair is:
   A. their eventual demise
   B. knowledge of good and evil
   C. painful childbirth
   D. hard labor to survive
   E. banishment from the garden

8. Adam's rib emphasizes his resulting:
   A. sacrifices for Eve
   B. bodily differentiation from Eve
   C. superiority to Eve
   D. defiance of God
   E. painful existence

9. As it turns out, the serpent:
   A. defies God
   B. has told the truth
   C. befriends the man and woman
   D. acts immorally
   E. is engulfed by thistles and thorns

10. Finally the Lord fears that man will also:
    A. take from the tree of life
    B. multiply his race
    C. become self-sufficient
    D. not respect Him
    E. enjoy sex

Genesis – Adam and Eve (circa 1500 BCE)

HOMER - THE ODYSSEY (800 BCE)

Cyclops episode Bk. IX

"We sailed hence, always in much distress, till we came to the land of the lawless and inhuman Cyclopes. Now the Cyclopes neither plant nor plough, but trust in providence, and live on such wheat, barley, and grapes as grow wild without any kind of tillage, and their wild grapes yield them wine as the sun and the rain may grow them. They have no laws nor assemblies of the people, but live in caves on the tops of high mountains; each is lord and master in his family, and they take no account of their neighbours.

"Now off their harbour there lies a wooded and fertile island not quite close to the land of the Cyclopes, but still not far. It is overrun with wild goats, that breed there in great numbers and are never disturbed by foot of man; for sportsmen- who as a rule will suffer so much hardship in forest or among mountain precipices- do not go there, nor yet again is it ever ploughed or fed down, but it lies a wilderness untilled and unsown from year to year, and has no living thing upon it but only goats. For the Cyclopes have no ships, nor yet shipwrights who could make ships for them; they cannot therefore go from city to city, or sail over the sea to one another's country as people who have ships can do; if they had had these they would have colonized the island, for it is a very good one, and would yield everything in due season. There are meadows that in some places come right down to the sea shore, well watered and full of luscious grass; grapes would do there excellently; there is level land for ploughing, and it would always yield heavily at harvest time, for the soil is deep. There is a good harbour where no cables are wanted, nor yet anchors, nor need a ship be moored, but all one has to do is to beach one's vessel and stay there till the wind becomes fair for putting out to sea again. At the head of the harbour there is a spring of clear water coming out of a cave, and there are poplars growing all round it.

"Here we entered, but so dark was the night that some god must have brought us in, for there was nothing whatever to be seen. A thick mist hung all round our ships; the moon was hidden behind a mass of clouds so that no one could have seen the island if he had looked for it, nor were there any breakers to tell us we were close in shore before we found ourselves upon the land itself; when, however, we had beached the ships, we took down the sails, went ashore and camped upon the beach till daybreak.

"When the child of morning, rosy-fingered Dawn, appeared, we admired the island and wandered all over it, while the nymphs Jove's daughters roused the wild goats that we might get some meat for our dinner. On this we fetched our spears and bows and arrows from the ships, and dividing ourselves into three bands began to shoot the goats. Heaven sent us excellent sport; I had twelve ships with me, and each ship got nine goats, while my own ship had ten; thus through the livelong day to the going down of the sun we ate and drank our fill,- and we had plenty of wine left, for each one of us had taken many jars full when we sacked the city of the Cicons, and this had not yet run out. While we were feasting we kept turning our eyes towards the land of the Cyclopes, which was hard by, and saw the smoke of their stubble fires. We could almost fancy we heard their voices and the bleating of their sheep and goats, but when the sun went down and it came on dark, we camped down upon the beach, and next morning I called a council.

"'Stay here, my brave fellows,' said I, 'all the rest of you, while I go with my ship and exploit these people myself: I want to see if they are uncivilized savages, or a hospitable and humane race.'

"I went on board, bidding my men to do so also and loose the hawsers; so they took their places and smote the grey sea with their oars. When we got to the land, which was not far, there, on the face of a cliff near the sea, we saw a great cave overhung with laurels. It was a station for a great many sheep and goats, and outside there was a large yard, with a high wall round it made of stones built into the ground and of trees both pine and oak. This was the abode of a huge monster who was then away from home shepherding his flocks. He would have nothing to do with other people, but led the life of an outlaw. He was a horrid creature, not like a human being at all, but resembling rather some crag that stands out boldly against the sky on the top of a high mountain.

"I told my men to draw the ship ashore, and stay where they were, all but the twelve best among them, who were to go along with myself. I also took a goatskin of sweet black wine which had been given me by Maron, Apollo son of Euanthes, who was priest of Apollo the patron god of Ismarus, and lived within the wooded precincts of the temple. When we were sacking the city we respected him, and spared his life, as also his wife and child; so he made me some presents of great value- seven talents of fine gold, and a bowl of silver, with twelve jars of sweet wine, unblended, and of the most exquisite flavour. Not a man nor maid in the house knew about it, but only himself, his wife, and one housekeeper: when he drank it he mixed twenty parts of water to one of wine, and yet the fragrance from the mixing-bowl was so exquisite that it was impossible to refrain from drinking. I filled a large skin with this wine, and took a wallet full of provisions with me, for my mind misgave me that I might have to deal with some savage who would be of great strength, and would respect neither right nor law.

"We soon reached his cave, but he was out shepherding, so we went inside and took stock of all that we could see. His cheeseracks were loaded with cheeses, and he had more lambs and kids than his pens could hold. They were kept in separate flocks; first there were the hoggets, then the oldest of the younger lambs and lastly the very young ones all kept apart from one another; as for his dairy, all the vessels, bowls, and milk pails into which he milked, were swimming with whey. When they saw all this, my men begged me to let them first steal some cheeses, and make off with them to the ship; they would then return, drive down the lambs and kids, put them on board and sail away with them. It would have been indeed better if we had done so but I would not listen to them, for I wanted to see the owner himself, in the hope that he might give me a present. When, however, we saw him my poor men found him ill to deal with.

"We lit a fire, offered some of the cheeses in sacrifice, ate others of them, and then sat waiting till the Cyclops should come in with his sheep. When he came, he brought in with him a huge load of dry firewood to light the fire for his supper, and this he flung with such a noise on to the floor of his cave that we hid ourselves for fear at the far end of the cavern. Meanwhile he drove all the ewes inside, as well as the she-goats that he was going to milk, leaving the males, both rams and he-goats, outside in the yards. Then he rolled a huge stone to the mouth of the cave- so huge that two and twenty strong four-wheeled waggons would not be enough to draw it from its place against the doorway. When he had so done he sat down and milked his ewes and goats, all in due course, and then let each of them have her own young. He curdled half the milk and set it aside in wicker strainers, but the other half he poured into bowls that he might drink it for his supper. When he had got through with all his work, he lit the fire, and then caught sight of us, whereon he said:

"'Strangers, who are you? Where do sail from? Are you traders, or do you sail the as rovers, with your hands against every man, and every man's hand against you?'

"We were frightened out of our senses by his loud voice and monstrous form, but I managed to say, 'We are Achaeans on our way home from Troy, but by the will of Jove, and stress of weather, we have been driven far out of our course. We are the people of Agamemnon, son of Atreus, who has won infinite renown throughout the whole world, by sacking so great a city and killing so many people. We therefore humbly pray you to show us some hospitality, and otherwise make us such presents as visitors may reasonably expect. May your excellency fear the wrath of heaven, for we are your suppliants, and Jove takes all respectable travellers under his protection, for he is the avenger of all suppliants and foreigners in distress.'

"To this he gave me but a pitiless answer, 'Stranger,' said he, 'you are a fool, or else you know nothing of this country. Talk to me, indeed, about fearing the gods or shunning their anger? We Cyclopes do not care about Jove or any of your blessed gods, for we are ever so much stronger than they. I shall not spare either yourself or your companions out of any regard for Jove, unless I am in the humour for doing so. And now tell me where you made your ship fast when you came on shore. Was it round the point, or is she lying straight off the land?'

"He said this to draw me out, but I was too cunning to be caught in that way, so I answered with a lie; 'Neptune,' said I, 'sent my ship on to the rocks at the far end of your country, and wrecked it. We were driven on to them from the open sea, but I and those who are with me escaped the jaws of death.'

"The cruel wretch vouchsafed me not one word of answer, but with a sudden clutch he gripped up two of my men at once and dashed them down upon the ground as though they had been puppies. Their brains were shed upon the ground, and the earth was wet with their blood. Then he tore them limb from limb and supped upon them. He gobbled them up like a lion in the wilderness, flesh, bones, marrow, and entrails, without leaving anything uneaten. As for us, we wept and lifted up our hands to heaven on seeing such a horrid sight, for we did not know what else to do; but when the Cyclops had filled his huge paunch, and had washed down his meal of human flesh with a drink of neat milk, he stretched himself full length upon the ground among his sheep, and went to sleep. I was at first inclined to seize my sword, draw it, and drive it into his vitals, but I reflected that if I did we should all certainly be lost, for we should never be able to shift the stone which the monster had put in front of the door. So we stayed sobbing and sighing where we were till morning came.

"When the child of morning, rosy-fingered Dawn, appeared, he again lit his fire, milked his goats and ewes, all quite rightly, and then let each have her own young one; as soon as he had got through with all his work, he clutched up two more of my men, and began eating them for his morning's meal. Presently, with the utmost ease, he rolled the stone away from the door and drove out his sheep, but he at once put it back again- as easily as though he were merely clapping the lid on to a quiver full of arrows. As soon as he had done so he shouted, and cried 'Shoo, shoo,' after his sheep to drive them on to the mountain; so I was left to scheme some way of taking my revenge and covering myself with glory.

"In the end I deemed it would be the best plan to do as follows. The Cyclops had a great club which was lying near one of the sheep pens; it was of green olive wood, and he had cut it intending to use it for a staff as soon as it should be dry. It was so huge that we could only compare it to the mast of a twenty-oared merchant vessel of large burden, and able to venture out into open sea. I went up to this club and cut off about six feet of it; I then gave this piece to the men and told them to fine it evenly off at one end, which they proceeded to do, and lastly I brought it to a point myself, charring the end in the fire to make it harder. When I had done this I hid it under dung, which was lying about all over the cave, and told the men to cast lots which of them should venture along with myself to lift it and bore it into the monster's eye while he was asleep. The lot fell upon the very four whom I should have chosen, and I myself made five. In the evening the wretch came back from shepherding, and drove his flocks into the cave- this time driving them all inside, and not leaving any in the yards; I suppose some fancy must have taken him, or a god must have prompted him to do so. As soon as he had put the stone back to its place against the door, he sat down, milked his ewes and his goats all quite rightly, and then let each have her own young one; when he had got through with all this work, he gripped up two more of my men, and made his supper off them. So I went up to him with an ivy-wood bowl of black wine in my hands:

"'Look here, Cyclops,' said I, you have been eating a great deal of man's flesh, so take this and drink some wine, that you may see what kind of liquor we had on board my ship. I was bringing it to you as a drink-offering, in the hope that you would take compassion upon me and further me on my way home, whereas all you do is to go on ramping and raving most intolerably. You ought to be ashamed yourself; how can you expect people to come see you any more if you treat them in this way?'

"He then took the cup and drank. He was so delighted with the taste of the wine that he begged me for another bowl full. 'Be so kind,' he said, 'as to give me some more, and tell me your name at once. I want to make you a present that you will be glad to have. We have wine even in this country, for our soil grows grapes and the sun ripens them, but this drinks like nectar and ambrosia all in one.'

"I then gave him some more; three times did I fill the bowl for him, and three times did he drain it without thought or heed; then, when I saw that the wine had got into his head, I said to him as plausibly as I could: 'Cyclops, you ask my name and I will tell it you; give me, therefore, the present you promised me; my name is Noman; this is what my father and mother and my friends have always called me.'

"But the cruel wretch said, 'Then I will eat all Noman's comrades before Noman himself, and will keep Noman for the last. This is the present that I will make him.'

As he spoke he reeled, and fell sprawling face upwards on the ground. His great neck hung heavily backwards and a deep sleep took hold upon him. Presently he turned sick, and threw up both wine and the gobbets of human flesh on which he had been gorging, for he was very drunk. Then I thrust the beam of wood far into the embers to heat it, and encouraged my men lest any of them should turn faint-hearted. When the wood, green though it was, was about to blaze, I drew it out of the fire glowing with heat, and my men gathered round me, for heaven had filled their hearts with courage. We drove the sharp end of the beam into the monster's eye, and bearing upon it with all my weight I kept turning it round and round as though I were boring a hole in a ship's plank with an auger, which two men with a wheel and strap can keep on turning as long as they choose. Even thus did we bore the red hot beam into his eye, till the boiling blood bubbled all over it as we worked it round and round, so that the steam from the burning eyeball scalded his eyelids and eyebrows, and the roots of the eye sputtered in the fire. As a blacksmith plunges an axe or hatchet into cold water to temper it- for it is this that gives strength to the iron- and it makes a great hiss as he does so, even thus did the Cyclops' eye hiss round the beam of olive wood, and his hideous yells made the cave ring again. We ran away in a fright, but he plucked the beam all besmirched with gore from his eye, and hurled it from him in a frenzy of rage and pain, shouting as he did so to the other Cyclopes who lived on the bleak headlands near him; so they gathered from all quarters round his cave when they heard him crying, and asked what was the matter with him.

"'What ails you, Polyphemus,' said they, 'that you make such a noise, breaking the stillness of the night, and preventing us from being able to sleep? Surely no man is carrying off your sheep? Surely no man is trying to kill you either by fraud or by force?

"But Polyphemus shouted to them from inside the cave, 'Noman is killing me by fraud! Noman is killing me by force!'

"'Then,' said they, 'if no man is attacking you, you must be ill; when Jove makes people ill, there is no help for it, and you had better pray to your father Neptune.'

"Then they went away, and I laughed inwardly at the success of my clever stratagem, but the Cyclops, groaning and in an agony of pain, felt about with his hands till he found the stone and took it from the door; then he sat in the doorway and stretched his hands in front of it to catch anyone going out with the sheep, for he thought I might be foolish enough to attempt this.

"As for myself I kept on puzzling to think how I could best save my own life and those of my companions; I schemed and schemed, as one who knows that his life depends upon it, for the danger was very great. In the end I deemed that this plan would be the best. The male sheep were well grown, and carried a heavy black fleece, so I bound them noiselessly in threes together, with some of the withies on which the wicked monster used to sleep. There was to be a man under the middle sheep, and the two on either side were to cover him, so that there were three sheep to each man. As for myself there was a ram finer than any of the others, so I caught hold of him by the back, esconced myself in the thick wool under his belly, and hung on patiently to his fleece, face upwards, keeping a firm hold on it all the time.

Thus, then, did we wait in great fear of mind till morning came, but when the child of morning, rosy-fingered Dawn, appeared, the male sheep hurried out to feed, while the ewes remained bleating about the pens waiting to be milked, for their udders were full to bursting; but their master in spite of all his pain felt the backs of all the sheep as they stood upright, without being sharp enough to find out that the men were underneath their bellies. As the ram was going out, last of all, heavy with its fleece and with the weight of my crafty self; Polyphemus laid hold of it and said:

"'My good ram, what is it that makes you the last to leave my cave this morning? You are not wont to let the ewes go before you, but lead the mob with a run whether to flowery mead or bubbling fountain, and are the first to come home again at night; but now you lag last of all. Is it because you know your master has lost his eye, and are sorry because that wicked Noman and his horrid crew have got him down in his drink and blinded him? But I will have his life yet. If you could understand and talk, you would tell me where the wretch is hiding, and I would dash his brains upon the ground till they flew all over the cave. I should thus have some satisfaction for the harm a this no-good Noman has done me.'

"As spoke he drove the ram outside, but when we were a little way out from the cave and yards, I first got from under the ram's belly, and then freed my comrades; as for the sheep, which were very fat, by constantly heading them in the right direction we managed to drive them down to the ship. The crew rejoiced greatly at seeing those of us who had escaped death, but wept for the others whom the Cyclops had killed. However, I made signs to them by nodding and frowning that they were to hush their crying, and told them to get all the sheep on board at once and put out to sea; so they went aboard, took their places, and smote the grey sea with their oars. Then, when I had got as far out as my voice would reach, I began to jeer at the Cyclops.

"'Cyclops,' said I, 'you should have taken better measure of your man before eating up his comrades in your cave. You wretch, eat up your visitors in your own house? You might have known that your sin would find you out, and now Jove and the other gods have punished you.'

"He got more and more furious as he heard me, so he tore the top from off a high mountain, and flung it just in front of my ship so that it was within a little of hitting the end of the rudder. The sea quaked as the rock fell into it, and the wash of the wave it raised carried us back towards the mainland, and forced us towards the shore. But I snatched up a long pole and kept the ship off, making signs to my men by nodding my head, that they must row for their lives, whereon they laid out with a will. When we had got twice as far as we were before, I was for jeering at the Cyclops again, but the men begged and prayed of me to hold my tongue.

"'Do not,' they exclaimed, 'be mad enough to provoke this savage creature further; he has thrown one rock at us already which drove us back again to the mainland, and we made sure it had been the death of us; if he had then heard any further sound of voices he would have pounded our heads and our ship's timbers into a jelly with the rugged rocks he would have heaved at us, for he can throw them a long way.'

"But I would not listen to them, and shouted out to him in my rage, 'Cyclops, if any one asks you who it was that put your eye out and spoiled your beauty, say it was the valiant warrior Ulysses, son of Laertes, who lives in Ithaca.'

"On this he groaned, and cried out, 'Alas, alas, then the old prophecy about me is coming true. There was a prophet here, at one time, a man both brave and of great stature, Telemus son of Eurymus, who was an excellent seer, and did all the prophesying for the Cyclopes till he grew old; he told me that all this would happen to me some day, and said I should lose my sight by the hand of Ulysses. I have been all along expecting some one of imposing presence and superhuman strength, whereas he turns out to be a little insignificant weakling, who has managed to blind my eye by taking advantage of me in my drink; come here, then, Ulysses, that I may make you presents to show my hospitality, and urge Neptune to help you forward on your journey- for Neptune and I are father and son. He, if he so will, shall heal me, which no one else neither god nor man can do.'

"Then I said, 'I wish I could be as sure of killing you outright and sending you down to the house of Hades, as I am that it will take more than Neptune to cure that eye of yours.'

"On this he lifted up his hands to the firmament of heaven and prayed, saying, 'Hear me, great Neptune; if I am indeed your own true-begotten son, grant that Ulysses may never reach his home alive; or if he must get back to his friends at last, let him do so late and in sore plight after losing all his men [let him reach his home in another man's ship and find trouble in his house.']

"Thus did he pray, and Neptune heard his prayer. Then he picked up a rock much larger than the first, swung it aloft and hurled it with prodigious force. It fell just short of the ship, but was within a little of hitting the end of the rudder. The sea quaked as the rock fell into it, and the wash of the wave it raised drove us onwards on our way towards the shore of the island.

"When at last we got to the island where we had left the rest of our ships, we found our comrades lamenting us, and anxiously awaiting our return. We ran our vessel upon the sands and got out of her on to the sea shore; we also landed the Cyclops' sheep, and divided them equitably amongst us so that none might have reason to complain. As for the ram, my companions agreed that I should have it as an extra share; so I sacrificed it on the sea shore, and burned its thigh bones to Jove, who is the lord of all. But he heeded not my sacrifice, and only thought how he might destroy my ships and my comrades.

"Thus through the livelong day to the going down of the sun we feasted our fill on meat and drink, but when the sun went down and it came on dark, we camped upon the beach. When the child of morning, rosy-fingered Dawn, appeared, I bade my men on board and loose the hawsers. Then they took their places and smote the grey sea with their oars; so we sailed on with sorrow in our hearts, but glad to have escaped death though we had lost our comrades.

Exercises

1. The Cyclopes survive through:
   A. reliance on their neighbors
   B. things growing wild
   C. eating their own produce
   D. raiding their neighbors
   E. milking their herds

2. After first landing the sailors feast on:
   A. food given from the Cyclopes
   B. sheep
   C. wild pigs
   D. wild goats
   E. cattle

3. The hero doesn't murder the sleeping Cyclops because Ulysses:
   A. fears the gods' retribution
   B. lacks an escape route
   C. fears arousing other Cyclopes
   D. lacks the required strength
   E. would rather humiliate the Cyclops

4. In all, the number of Ulysses' men falling victim to the Cyclops is:
   A. not stated
   B. two
   C. four
   D. six
   E. eight

5. Ulysses's trickery involves all except:
   A. lies about his ship
   B. a made-up prophecy
   C. a phony name
   D. using wine as a weapon
   E. hiding under an animal

6. Polyphemus claims he will:
   A. maroon Ulysses
   B. have Zeus heal his wounded eye
   C. kill the prophet who foresaw this fate
   D. sink Ulysses's ship
   E. enlist his father, Neptune, for a storm

7. The Ulysses is most notably characterized by his:
   A. strength
   B. cleverness
   C. homesickness
   D. courage
   E. thirst for glory

8. This story is best described as a:
   A. fable
   B. myth
   C. fairy tale
   D. morality tale
   E. legend

9. Ulysses most regrets:
   A. not killing the Cyclops
   B. absence from home
   C. lost shipmates
   D. losing the ship's rudder
   E. angering the gods

10. The author presents Ulysses' actions as:
    A. foolhardy
    B. heroic
    C. impolite
    D. risky
    E. cruel

MIGUEL CERVANTES - DON QUIXOTE (1605)

Windmills

At this point they came in sight of thirty or forty windmills that are on that plain.

"Fortune," said Don Quixote to his squire, as soon as he had seen them, "is arranging matters for us better than we could have hoped. Look there, friend Sancho Panza, where thirty or more monstrous giants rise up, all of whom I mean to engage in battle and slay, and with whose spoils we shall begin to make our fortunes. For this is righteous warfare, and it is God's good service to sweep so evil a breed from off the face of the earth."

"What giants?" said Sancho Panza.

"Those you see there," answered his master, "with the long arms, and some have them nearly two leagues long."

"Look, your worship," said Sancho. "What we see there are not giants but windmills, and what seem to be their arms are the vanes that turned by the wind make the millstone go."

"It is easy to see," replied Don Quixote, "that you are not used to this business of adventures. Those are giants, and if you are afraid, away with you out of here and betake yourself to prayer, while I engage them in fierce and unequal combat."

So saying, he gave the spur to his steed Rocinante, heedless of the cries his squire Sancho sent after him, warning him that most certainly they were windmills and not giants he was going to attack. He, however, was so positive they were giants that he neither heard the cries of Sancho, nor perceived, near as he was, what they were.

"Fly not, cowards and vile beings," he shouted, "for a single knight attacks you."

A slight breeze at this moment sprang up, and the great vanes began to move.

"Though ye flourish more arms than the giant Briareus, ye have to reckon with me!" exclaimed Don Quixote, when he saw this.

So saying, he commended himself with all his heart to his lady Dulcinea, imploring her to support him in such a peril. With lance braced and covered by his shield, he charged at Rocinante's fullest gallop and attacked the first mill that stood in front of him. But as he drove his lance-point into the sail, the wind whirled it around with such force that it shivered the lance to pieces. It swept away with it horse and rider, and they were sent rolling over the plain, in sad condition indeed.

Sancho hastened to his assistance as fast as the ass could go. When he came up and found Don Quixote unable to move, with such an impact had Rocinante fallen with him.

"God Bless me!," said Sancho, "did I not tell your worship to watch what you were doing, because they were only windmills? No one could have made any mistake about it unless he had something of the same kind in his head."

"Silence, friend Sancho," replied Don Quixote. "The fortunes of war more than any other are liable to frequent fluctuations. Moreover I think, and it is the truth, that the same sage Frestón who carried off my study and books, has turned these giants into mills in order to rob me of the glory of vanquishing them, such is the enmity he bears me. But in the end his wicked arts will avail but little against my good sword."

"God's will be done," said Sancho Panza, and helping him to rise got him again on Rocinante, whose shoulder was half dislocated. Then, discussing the adventure, they followed the road to Puerto Lápice, for there, said Don Quixote, they could not fail to find adventures in abundance and variety, as it was a well-traveled thoroughfare.

For all that, he was much grieved at the loss of his lance, and said so to his squire.

"I remember having read," he added, "how a Spanish knight, Diego Pérez de Vargas by name, having broken his sword in battle, tore from an oak a ponderous bough or branch. With it he did such things that day, and pounded so many Moors, that he got the surname of Machuca and his descendants from that day forth are called Vargas y Machuca. I mention this because from the first oak I see I mean to tear a branch, large and stout. I am determined and resolved to do such deeds with it that you may deem yourself very fortunate in being found worthy to see them and be an eyewitness of things that will scarcely be believed."

"Be that as God wills," said Sancho, "I believe it all as your worship says it. But straighten yourself a little, for you seem to be leaning to one side, maybe from the shaking you got when you fell."

"That is the truth, said Don Quixote, "and if I make no complaint of the pain it is because knights-errant are not permitted to complain of any wound, even though their bowels be coming out through it."

"If so," said Sancho, "I have nothing to say. But God knows I would rather your worship complained when anything ailed you. For my part, I confess I must complain however small the ache may be, unless this rule about not complaining applies to the squires of knights-errant also."

Don Quixote could not help laughing at his squire's simplicity, and assured him he might complain whenever and however he chose, just as he liked. So far he had never read of anything to the contrary in the order of knighthood.

Sancho reminded him it was dinner time, to which his master answered that he wanted nothing himself just then, but that Sancho might eat when he had a mind. With this permission Sancho settled himself as com-

fortably as he could on his beast, and taking out of the saddlebags what he had stowed away in them, he jogged along behind his master munching slowly. From time to time
135 he took a pull at the wineskin with all the enjoyment that the thirstiest tavern-keeper in Málaga might have envied. And while he went on in this way, between gulps, he never gave a thought to any of the promises his
140 master had made him, nor did he rate it as hardship but rather as recreation going in quest of adventures, however dangerous they might be.

Finally they settled down for the night
145 among some trees. From one of them Don Quixote plucked a dry branch to serve as a lance, fixing on it the head he had removed from the broken one. All that night Don Quixote lay awake thinking of his lady
150 Dulcinea, in conformity with what he had read in his books, how many a night in the forests and deserts knights used to lie sleepless, borne up by the memory of their mistresses.

155 Sancho Panza spent it thus: having his stomach full of something stronger than chicory water he slept straight through. If his master had not called him, neither the rays of the sun beating on his face nor all
160 the cheery notes of the birds welcoming the approach of day would have had power to waken him.

Miguel Cervantes - Don Quixote (1605)

Exercises

1. Quixote's ideas of knighthood come from:
   A. fellow knights
   B. Sancho
   C. local legend
   D. books
   E. Dulcinea

2. Quixote seems to believe in all the following except:
   A. the devil
   B. fortune
   C. evil
   D. God
   E. giants

3. Quixote blames his loss in the windmill joust on:
   A. an unfair fight
   B. an inadequate lance
   C. ill-considered tactics
   D. wicked arts
   E. bad luck

4. Quixote's says his central quest is for:
   A. an eventual coming to rest
   B. adventure
   C. a woman's love
   D. truth
   E. fame

5. Sancho, in contrast to Quixote, is described as:
   A. chivalrous
   B. lazy
   C. pessimistic
   D. a guiding force
   E. a realist

6. Quixote exemplifies his chivalric code in all the following ways except his indifference to:
   A. women
   B. meals
   C. pain
   D. comfort
   E. sleep

7. Sancho personally thinks of their joint travels as:
   A. a hardship
   B. an amusing joke
   C. a form of recreation
   D. dangerous
   E. a great fantasy

8. A best synonym for "quixotic", describing the main character, is:
   A. silly
   B. starry-eyed
   C. imaginative
   D. gentlemanly
   E. heroic

9. Quixote says a true knight must:
   A. not complain of pain
   B. fight alone
   C. have a mistress
   D. stay astride his horse
   E. stay awake

10. Squire Sancho is aroused from his wine-induced slumber by:
    A. the sun's rays
    B. chirping birds
    C. Rocinante
    D. Dulcinea
    E. Quixote

GRIMM BROTHERS – CINDERELLA (1812)

The wife of a rich man fell sick, and as she felt that her end was drawing near, she called her only daughter to her bedside and said, "Dear child, be good and pious, and then the good God will always protect thee, and I will look down on thee from heaven and be near thee." Thereupon she closed her eyes and departed. Every day the maiden went out to her mother's grave, and wept, and she remained pious and good. When winter came the snow spread a white sheet over the grave, and when the spring sun had drawn it off again, the man had taken another wife.

The woman had brought two daughters into the house with her, who were beautiful and fair of face, but vile and black of heart. Now began a bad time for the poor stepchild. "Is the stupid goose to sit in the parlour with us?" said they. "He who wants to eat bread must earn it; out with the kitchen-wench." They took her pretty clothes away from her, put an old grey bedgown on her, and gave her wooden shoes. "Just look at the proud princess, how decked out she is!" they cried, and laughed, and led her into the kitchen. There she had to do hard work from morning till night, get up before daybreak, carry water, light fires, cook and wash. Besides this, the sisters did her every imaginable injury -- they mocked her and emptied her peas and lentils into the ashes, so that she was forced to sit and pick them out again. In the evening when she had worked till she was weary she had no bed to go to, but had to sleep by the fireside in the ashes. And as on that account she always looked dusty and dirty, they called her Cinderella. It happened that the father was once going to the fair, and he asked his two step-daughters what he should bring back for them. "Beautiful dresses," said one, "Pearls and jewels," said the second. "And thou, Cinderella," said he, "what wilt thou have?" "Father, break off for me the first branch which knocks against your hat on your way home." So he bought beautiful dresses, pearls and jewels for his two step-daughters, and on his way home, as he was riding through a green thicket, a hazel twig brushed against him and knocked off his hat. Then he broke off the branch and took it with him. When he reached home he gave his step-daughters the things which they had wished for, and to Cinderella he gave the branch from the hazel-bush. Cinderella thanked him, went to her mother's grave and planted the branch on it, and wept so much that the tears fell down on it and watered it. And it grew, however, and became a handsome tree. Thrice a day Cinderella went and sat beneath it, and wept and prayed, and a little white bird always came on the tree, and if Cinderella expressed a wish, the bird threw down to her what she had wished for.

It happened, however, that the King appointed a festival which was to last three days, and to which all the beautiful young girls in the country were invited, in order that his son might choose himself a bride. When the two step-sisters heard that they too were to appear among the number, they were delighted, called Cinderella and said, "Comb our hair for us, brush our shoes and fasten our buckles, for we are going to the festival at the King's palace." Cinderella obeyed, but wept, because she too would have liked to go with them to the dance, and begged her step-mother to allow her to do so. "Thou go, Cinderella!" said she; "Thou art dusty and dirty and wouldst go to the festival? Thou hast no clothes and shoes, and yet wouldst dance!" As, however, Cinderella went on asking, the step-mother at last said, "I have emptied a dish of lentils into the ashes for thee, if thou hast picked them out again in two hours, thou shalt go with us." The maiden went through the back-door into the garden, and called, "You tame pigeons, you turtle-doves, and all you birds beneath the sky, come and help me to pick

"The good into the pot,
The bad into the crop."

Then two white pigeons came in by the kitchen-window, and afterwards the turtle-doves, and at last all the birds beneath the sky, came whirring and crowding in, and alighted amongst the ashes. And the pigeons nodded with their heads and began pick, pick, pick, pick, and the rest began also pick, pick, pick, pick, and gathered all the good grains into the dish. Hardly had one hour passed before they had finished, and all flew out again. Then the girl took the dish to her step-mother, and was glad, and believed that now she would be allowed to go with them to the festival. But the step-mother said, "No, Cinderella, thou hast no clothes and thou canst not dance; thou wouldst only be laughed at." And as Cinderella wept at this, the step-mother said, "If thou canst pick two dishes of lentils out of the ashes for me in one hour, thou shalt go with us." And she thought to herself, "That she most certainly cannot do." When the step-mother had emptied the two dishes of lentils amongst the ashes, the maiden went through the back-door into the garden and cried, You tame pigeons, you turtle-doves, and all you birds under heaven, come and help me to pick

"The good into the pot,
The bad into the crop."

Then two white pigeons came in by the kitchen-window, and afterwards the turtle-doves, and at length all the birds beneath the sky, came whirring and crowding in, and alighted amongst the ashes. And the doves nodded with their heads and began pick, pick, pick, pick, and the others began also pick, pick, pick, pick, and gathered all the good seeds into the dishes, and before half an hour was over they had already finished, and all flew out again. Then the maiden carried the dishes to the step-mother and was delighted, and believed that she might now go with them to the festival. But the step-mother said, "All this will not help thee; thou goest not with us, for thou hast no clothes and canst not dance; we should be ashamed of thee!" On this she turned her back on Cinderella, and hurried away with her two proud daughters.

As no one was now at home, Cinderella went to her mother's grave beneath the hazel-tree, and cried,

"Shiver and quiver, little tree,
Silver and gold throw down over me."

Then the bird threw a gold and silver dress down to her, and slippers embroidered with silk and silver. She put on the dress with all speed, and went to the festival. Her step-sisters and the step-mother however did not know her, and thought she must be a foreign princess, for she looked so beautiful in the golden dress. They never once thought of Cinderella, and believed that she was sitting at home in the dirt, picking lentils out of the ashes. The prince went to meet her, took her by the hand and danced with her. He would dance with no other maiden, and never left loose of her hand, and if any one else came to invite her, he said, "This is my partner."

She danced till it was evening, and then she wanted to go home. But the King's son said, "I will go with thee and bear thee company," for he wished to see to whom the beautiful maiden belonged. She escaped from him, however, and sprang into the pigeon-house. The King's son waited until her father came, and then he told him that the stranger maiden had leapt into the pigeon-house. The old man thought, "Can it be Cinderella?" and they had to bring him an axe and a pickaxe that he might hew the pigeon-house to pieces, but no one was inside it. And when they got home Cinderella lay in her dirty clothes among the ashes, and a dim little oil-lamp was burning on the mantle-piece, for Cinderella had jumped quickly down from the back of the pigeon-house and had run to the little hazel-tree, and there she had taken off her beautiful clothes and laid them on the grave, and the bird had taken them away again, and then she had placed herself in the kitchen amongst the ashes in her grey gown.

Next day when the festival began afresh, and her parents and the step-sisters had gone once more, Cinderella went to the hazel-tree and said --

"Shiver and quiver, my little tree,
Silver and gold throw down over me."

Then the bird threw down a much more beautiful dress than on the preceding day. And when Cinderella appeared at the festival in this dress, every one was astonished at her beauty. The King's son had waited until she came, and instantly took her by the hand and danced with no one but her. When others came and invited her, he said, "She is my partner." When evening came she wished to leave, and the King's son followed her and wanted to see into which house she went. But she sprang away from him, and into the garden behind the house. Therein stood a beautiful tall tree on which hung the most magnificent pears. She clambered so nimbly between the branches like a squirrel that the King's son did not know where she was gone. He waited until her father came, and said to him, "The stranger-maiden has escaped from me, and I believe she has climbed up the pear-tree." The father thought, "Can it be Cinderella?" and had an axe brought and cut the tree down, but no one was on it. And when they got into the kitchen, Cinderella lay there amongst the ashes, as usual, for she had jumped down on the other side of the tree, had taken the beautiful dress to the bird on the little hazel-tree, and put on her grey gown.

On the third day, when the parents and sisters had gone away, Cinderella went once more to her mother's grave and said to the little tree --

"Shiver and quiver, my little tree,
Silver and gold throw down over me."

And now the bird threw down to her a dress which was more splendid and magnificent than any she had yet had, and the slippers were golden. And when she went to the festival in the dress, no one knew how to speak for astonishment. The King's son danced with her only, and if any one invited her to dance, he said, "She is my partner."

When evening came, Cinderella wished to leave, and the King's son was anxious to go with her, but she escaped from him so quickly that he could not follow her. The King's son had, however, used a strategem, and had caused the whole staircase to be smeared with pitch, and there, when she ran down, had the maiden's left slipper remained sticking. The King's son picked it up, and it was small and dainty, and all golden. Next morning, he went with it to the father, and said to him, "No one shall be my wife but she whose foot this golden slipper fits." Then were the two sisters glad, for they had pretty feet. The eldest went with the shoe into her room and wanted to try it on, and her mother stood by. But she could not get her big toe into it, and the shoe was too small for her. Then her mother gave her a knife and said, "Cut the toe off; when thou art Queen thou wilt have no more need to go on foot." The maiden cut the toe off, forced the foot into the shoe, swallowed the pain, and went out to the King's son. Then he took her on his his horse as his bride and rode away with her. They were, however, obliged to pass the grave, and there, on the hazel-tree, sat the two pigeons and cried,

"Turn and peep, turn and peep,
There's blood within the shoe,
The shoe it is too small for her,
The true bride waits for you."

Then he looked at her foot and saw how the blood was streaming from it. He turned his horse round and took the false bride home again, and said she was not the true one, and that the other sister was to put the shoe on. Then this one went into her chamber and got her toes safely into the shoe, but her heel was too large. So her mother gave her a knife and said, "Cut a bit off thy heel; when thou art Queen thou wilt have no more need to go on foot." The maiden cut a bit off her heel, forced her foot into the shoe, swallowed the pain, and went out to the King's son. He took her on his horse as his bride, and rode away with her, but when they passed by the hazel-tree, two little pigeons sat on it and cried,

"Turn and peep, turn and peep,
There's blood within the shoe
The shoe it is too small for her,
The true bride waits for you."

He looked down at her foot and saw how the blood was running out of her shoe, and how it had stained her white stocking. Then he turned his horse and took the false bride home again. "This also is not the right one," said he, "have you no other daughter?" "No," said the man, "There is still a little stunted kitchen-wench which my late wife left behind her, but she cannot possibly be the bride." The King's son said he was to send her up to him; but the mother answered, "Oh, no, she is much too dirty, she cannot show herself!" He absolutely insisted on it, and Cinderella had to be called. She first washed her hands and face clean, and then went and bowed down before the King's son, who gave her the golden shoe. Then she seated herself on a stool, drew her foot out of the heavy wooden shoe, and put it into the slipper, which fitted like a glove. And when she rose up and the King's son looked at her face he recognized the beautiful maiden who had danced with him and cried, "That is the true bride!" The stepmother and the two sisters were terrified and became pale with rage; he, however, took Cinderella on his horse and rode away with her. As they passed by the hazel-tree, the two white doves cried --

"Turn and peep, turn and peep,
No blood is in the shoe,
The shoe is not too small for her,
The true bride rides with you,"

and when they had cried that, the two came flying down and placed themselves on Cinderella's shoulders, one on the right, the other on the left, and remained sitting there.

When the wedding with the King's son had to be celebrated, the two false sisters came and wanted to get into favour with Cinderella and share her good fortune. When the betrothed couple went to church, the elder was at the right side and the younger at the left, and the pigeons pecked out one eye of each of them. Afterwards as they came back, the elder was at the left, and the younger at the right, and then the pigeons pecked out the other eye of each. And thus, for their wickedness and falsehood, they were punished with blindness as long as they lived.

Grimm brothers – Cinderella (1812)

Exercises

1. Cinderella got her name from her:
   A. father
   B. mother
   C. stepmother
   D. sleeping place
   E. bare feet

2. Cinderella's stepsisters are all of the following except:
   A. ambitious
   B. beautiful
   C. bossy
   D. ridiculing
   E. vain

3. The twig Cinderella requests from her father results in:
   A. her sisters' mockery
   B. her sisters' envy
   C. a fruit-bearing tree
   D. a willow tree
   E. a bird's appearance

4. Cinderella is told she can't attend the dance for all the following reasons except:
   A. she would shame the family
   B. she'd be laughed at
   C. she is dirty
   D. she lacks a pretty face
   E. she hasn't proper shoes

5. Cinderella's father brings home all of the following except:
   A. a bird
   B. pearls
   C. a twig
   D. dresses
   E. jewels

6. Cinderella's father does all of the following except:
   A. fells a tree
   B. smashes a bird house
   C. gives jewels to a step-daughter
   D. visits his widow's grave
   E. treats his daughters well

7. Compared to the Disney version, the Grimms' "Cinderella" contains:
   A. more humor
   B. more trickery
   C. a more sympathetic heroine
   D. more violence
   E. more realism

8. A stairway is smeared with pitch by:
   A. the stepsisters
   B. the stepmother
   C. the father
   D. the prince
   E. birds

9. In fairy tales things come in threes. The exception in "Cinderella" is the number of:
   A. the festival days
   B. Cinderella's gowns
   C. rhymes sung by the birds
   D. stepsisters' tasks for Cinderella
   E. dishes of lentils

10. The stepsisters are punished by:
    A. the prince
    B. the stepfather
    C. the stepmother
    D. pigeons
    E. they go unpunished

Grimm brothers – Cinderella (1812)

Anton Chekhov – A Slander (1883)

Serge Kapitonich Ahineev, the writing master, was marrying his daughter to the teacher of history and geography. The wedding festivities were going off most successfully. In the drawing room there was singing, playing, and dancing. Waiters hired from the club were flitting distractedly about the rooms, dressed in black swallowtails and dirty white ties. There was a continual hubub and din of conversation. Sitting side by side on the sofa, the teacher of mathematics, the French teacher, and the junior assessor of taxes were talking hurriedly and interrupting one another as they described to the guests cases of persons being buried alive, and gave their opinions on spiritualism. None of them believed in spiritualism, but all admitted that there were many things in this world which would always be beyond the mind of man. In the next room the literature master was explaining to the visitors the cases in which a sentry has the right to fire on passers-by. The subjects, as you perceive, were alarming, but very agreeable. Persons whose social position precluded them from entering were looking in at the windows from the yard.

Just at midnight the master of the house went into the kitchen to see whether everything was ready for supper. The kitchen from floor to ceiling was filled with fumes composed of goose, duck, and many other odors. On two tables the accessories, the drinks and light refreshments, were set out in artistic disorder. The cook, Marfa, a red-faced woman whose figure was like a barrel with a belt around it, was bustling about the tables.

"Show me the sturgeon, Marfa," said Ahineev, rubbing his hands and licking his lips. "What a perfume! I could eat up the whole kitchen. Come, show me the sturgeon."

Marfa went up to one of the benches and cautiously lifted a piece of greasy newspaper. Under the paper on an immense dish there reposed a huge sturgeon, masked in jelly and decorated with capers, olives, and carrots. Ahineev gazed at the sturgeon and gasped. His face beamed, he turned his eyes up. He bent down and with his lips emitted the sound of an ungreased wheel. After standing a moment he snapped his fingers with delight and once more smacked his lips.

"Ah-ah! the sound of a passionate kiss.... Who is it you're kissing out there, little Marfa?" came a voice from the next room, and in the doorway there appeared the cropped head of the assistant usher, Vankin. "Who is it? A-a-h! ... Delighted to meet you! Sergei Kapitonich! You're a fine grandfather, I must say!"

"I'm not kissing," said Ahineev in confusion. "Who told you so, you fool? I was only ... I smacked my lips ... in reference to ... as an indication of... pleasure ... at the sight of the fish."

"Tell that to the marines!" The intrusive face vanished, wearing a broad grin.

Ahineev flushed.

"Hang it!" he thought, "the beast will go now and talk scandal. He'll disgrace me to all the town, the brute."

Ahineev went timidly into the drawing room and looked stealthily round for Vankin. Vankin was standing by the piano, and, bending down with a jaunty air, was whispering something to the inspector's sister-in-law, who was laughing.

"Talking about me!" thought Ahineev. "About me, blast him! And she believes it ... believes it! She laughs! Mercy on us! No, I can't let it pass ... I can't. I must do something to prevent his being believed.... I'll speak to them all, and he'll be shown up for a fool and a gossip."

Ahineev scratched his head, and still overcome with embarrassment, went up to the French teacher.

"I've just been in the kitchen to see after the supper," he said to the Frenchman. "I know you are fond of fish, and I've a sturgeon, my dear fellow, beyond everything! A yard and a half long! Ha, ha, ha! And, by the way ... I was just forgetting.... In the kitchen just now, with that sturgeon ... quite a little story! I went into the kitchen just now and wanted to look at the supper dishes. I looked at the sturgeon and I smacked my lips with relish ... at the piquancy of it. And at the very moment that fool Vankin came in and said: ... 'Ha, ha, ha! ... So you're kissing here!' Kissing Marfa, the cook! What a thing to imagine, silly fool! The woman is a perfect fright, like all the beasts put together, and he talks about kissing! Queer fish!"

"Who's a queer fish?" asked the mathematics teacher, coming up.

"Why he, over there--Vankin! I went into the kitchen ..."

And he told the story of Vankin. "... He amused me, queer fish! I'd rather kiss a dog than Marfa, if you ask me," added Ahineev. He looked round and saw behind him the junior assessor of taxes.

"We were talking of Vankin," he said. "Queer fish, he is! He went into the kitchen, saw me beside Marfa, and began inventing all sorts of silly stories. 'Why are you kissing?' he says. He must have had a drop too much. 'And I'd rather kiss a turkeycock than Marfa,' I said, 'And I've a wife of my own, you fool,' said I. He did amuse me!"

"Who amused you?" asked the priest who taught Scripture in the school, going up to Ahineev.

"Vankin. I was standing in the kitchen, you know, looking at the sturgeon...."

And so on. Within half an hour or so all the guests knew the incident of the sturgeon and Vankin.

"Let him tell away now!" thought Ahineev, rubbing his hands. "Let him! He'll begin telling his story and they'll say to him at once, 'Enough of your improbable nonsense, you fool, we know all about it!"

And Ahineev was so relieved that in his joy he drank four glasses too many. After escorting the young people to their room, he went to bed and slept like an innocent babe, and next day he thought no more of the incident with the sturgeon. But, alas! man proposes, but God disposes. An evil tongue did its evil work, and Ahineev's strategy was of no avail. Just a week later--to be precise, on Wednesday after the third lesson--when Ahineev was standing in the middle of the teacher's room, holding forth on the vicious propensities of a boy called Visekin, the headmaster went up to him and drew him aside:

"Look here, Sergei Kapitonich," said the headmaster, "you must excuse me. . . . It's not my business; but all the same I must make you realize. . . . It's my duty. You see, there are rumors that you are romancing with that . . . cook. . . . It's nothing to do with me, but . . . flirt with her, kiss her . . . as you please, but don't let it be so public, please. I entreat you! Don't forget that you're a schoolmaster."

Ahineev turned cold and faint. He went home like a man stung by a whole swarm of bees, like a man scalded with boiling water. As he walked home, it seemed to him that the whole town was looking at him as though he were smeared with pitch. At home fresh trouble awaited him.

"Why aren't you gobbling up your food as usual?" his wife asked him at dinner. "What are you so pensive about? Brooding over your amours? Pining for your Marfa? I know all about it, Mohammedan! Kind friends have opened my eyes! O-o-o! . . . you savage !"

And she slapped him in the face. He got up from the table, not feeling the earth under his feet, and without his hat or coat, made his way to Vankin. He found him at home.

"You scoundrel!" he addressed him. "Why have you covered me with mud before all the town? Why did you set this slander going about me?"

"What slander? What are you talking about?"

"Who was it gossiped of my kissing Marfa? Wasn't it you? Tell me that. Wasn't it you, you brigand?"

Vankin blinked and twitched in every fiber of his battered countenance, raised his eyes to the icon and articulated, "God blast me! Strike me blind and lay me out, if I said a single word about you! May I be left without house and home, may I be stricken with worse than cholera!"

Vankin's sincerity did not admit of doubt. It was evidently not he who was the author of the slander.

"But who, then, who?" Ahineev wondered, going over all his acquaintances in his mind and beating himself on the breast. "Who, then?"

Who, then? We, too, ask the reader.

Anton Chekhov – A Slander (1883)

Exercises

1. In line 24, the guests' conversation is described as "alarming" to suggest:
   A. the loudness of the chatter
   B. the excitement of the wedding
   C. numbers of tipsy party guests
   D. people arguing heatedly
   E. the guests' bizarre topics

2. The topics of discussion among Ahineev's guests include:
   A. how the waiters are dressed
   B. unfair taxes
   C. being buried alive
   D. the wedding festivities
   E. small talk

3. What does Ahineev find "amusing"?
   A. Marfa
   B. Vander
   C. the sturgeon
   D. rumors of a kiss
   E. the chatter of the guests

4. Ahineev's retelling the fish story is to:
   A. spread amusement among the guests
   B. lighten the party atmosphere
   C. annoy Vandin
   D. discredit the cook
   E. protect his reputation

5. He drinks at evening's end because he:
   A. is relieved the wedding's over
   B. wants to relax after the kiss business
   C. is upset at the evening's events
   D. is happy with his efforts
   E. wants to forget the fish incident

6. His boss criticizes Ahineev for:
   A. creating rumors and gossip
   B. unprofessional rudeness
   C. mocking his superiors
   D. romancing the cook
   E. apparent immorality

7. The tone of the story is:
   A. romantic
   B. mocking
   C. sentimental
   D. snobbish
   E. condemning

8. Ahineev and the groom are:
   A. neighbors
   B. clerks
   C. teachers
   D. dignitaries
   E. cooks

9. The slander was started by:
   A. Ahineev
   B. Marfa
   C. Vander
   D. the Frenchman
   E. the sturgeon

10. Ahineev's wife berates him, insinuating that her husband is a:
    A. beastly
    B. clown
    C. Moslem
    D. child
    E. busybody

English Literature

Sir Thomas Malory - Morte D'Arthur (1485)

SIR THOMAS MALORY - MORTE D'ARTHUR (1485)

Than the kynge dremed a mervaylous dreme whereof he was sore adrad. (But all thys tyme kynge Arthure knew nat kynge Lottis wyff was his sister.) But thus was the
5 dreme of Arthure: hym thought there was com into hys londe gryffens and serpentes, and hym thought they brent and slowghe all the people in the londe; and than he thought he fought with them and they dud hym
10 grete harme and wounded hym full sore, but at the laste he slew hem.

Whan the kynge waked, he was passynge hevy of hys dreme; and so to putte hit oute of thought he made hym redy with many
15 knyghtes to ryde on huntynge. And as sone as he was in the foreste, the kynge say a grete harte before hym. "Thys harte woll I chace," seyde kynge Arthure. And so he spurred hys horse and rode aftir longe, and
20 so be fyne force oftyn he was lyke to have smytten the herte. Wherefore as the kynge had chased the herte so longe that hys horse lost his brethe and felle downe dede, than a yoman fette the kynge another horse.

25 So the kynge was the herte unboced and hys horse dede, he sette hym downe by a fowntayne, and there he felle downe in grete thought. And as he sate so hym thought he herde a noyse of howundis to
30 the som of thirty, and with that the kynge saw com towarde hym the strongeste beste that ever he saw or herde of. So thys beste wente to the welle and dranke, and the noyse was in the bestes bealy lyke unto the
35 questyng of thirty coupyl houndres, but alle the whyle the beest dranke there was no noise in the bestes bealy. And therewith the beeste departed with a grete noyse, whereof the kynge had grete mervayle. And so he
40 was in a grete thought, and therewith he felle on slepe...

Thenne the kynge sat in a study and bade hys men fecche another horse as fast as they myght. Ryght so com by hym Merlyon
45 lyke a chylde of fourtene yere of ayge and salewed the kynge and asked hym whye he was so pensyff.

Sir Thomas Malory - Morte D'Arthur (1485)

"I may well be pensiff," seyde the kynge, "for I have sene the mervaylist syght that ever I saw."

"That know I well," seyde Merlyon, "as welle as thyselff, and of all thy thoughtes. But thou arte a foole to take thought for hit that woll nat amende the. Also I know what thou arte, and who was thy fadir, and of whom thou were begotyn: for kynge Uther was thy fadir and begate the on Igrayne."

"That ys false!" seyde kynge Arthure. "How sholdist thou know hit, for thou arte nat so olde of yerys to know my fadir?"

"Yes," seyde Merlyon, "I know hit bettir than ye or ony man lyvynge."

"I woll nat beleve the," seyde Arthure, and was wrothe with the chylde.

So departed Merlyon, and com ayen in the lyknesse of an olde man of four score yere of ayge, whereof the kynge was passynge glad, for he semed to be ryght wyse. Than seyde the olde man,

"Why ar ye so sad?"

"I may well be sad," seyde Arthure, "for many thynhes. For ryght now there was a chylde here, and tolde me many thynghes that mesemyth he sholde nat knowe, for he was nat of ayge to know my fadir."

"Yes," seyde the olde man, "the chylde tolde you trouthe, and more he wolde a tolde you and ye wolde a suffirde hym. But ye have done a thynge late that God ys displesed with you, for ye have lyene by youre syster and on hir ye have gotyn a childe that shall destroy you and all the knyghtes of youre realme."

"What are ye," seyde Arthure, "that telle me thys tydyngis?"

"Sir, I am Merlion, and I was he in the chyldis lycknes."

"A," seyde the kynge, "ye are a mervaylous man! But I mervayle muche of thy wordis that I mou dye in batayle."

"Mervayle nat," seyde Merlion, "for hit ys Goddis wylle that youre body sholde be punyssed for your fowle dedis. But I ought ever to be hevy," seyde Merlion, "for i shall dye a shamefull dethe, to be putte in the erthe quycke; and ye shall dey a worshipfull dethe."

And as they talked thus, com one with the kyngis horse, and so the kynge mownted on hys horse, and Merlion on anothir, and so rode unto Carlyon.

Sir Thomas Malory - Morte D'Arthur (1485)

Exercises

1. In Arthure's dream, all of the following happens except:
   A. Arthure learns the fate of his sister
   B. Arthure is wounded
   C. griffins enter the kingdom
   D. monsters kill people
   E. the king kills all the monsters

2. In the course of the hunt:
   A. Arthure's knights desert him
   B. Arthure smites the hart
   C. the hart disappears
   D. Arthure's horse breaks a leg
   E. Arthure rides his horse to death

3. The word "pensyff" ['pensive'] lines 47-48 most nearly means:
   A. lonely
   B. thoughtful
   C. amazed
   D. depressed
   E. bored

4. First seeing Arthure, Merlin says he knows all of the following about Arthure except:
   A. the marvel he's just seen
   B. his character
   C. his parentage
   D. his sister
   E. everything he's thinking

5. Arthure's reaction when Merlin first appears involves all the following except:
   A. ridicule
   B. anger
   C. non-recognition
   D. disbelief
   E. subsequent sadness

6. Arthure's "foul deed" in the sight of God was:
   A. dismissing the "chylde"
   B. killing
   C. putting his knights at risk
   D. incest
   E. fathering an illegitimate child

7. Arthure's prophesized death will be caused by:
   A. a knight's betrayal
   B. an angry God
   C. his bastard son
   D. Merlin
   E. being buried alive

8. Merlin predicts that he himself will die:
   A. in battle
   B. in bed
   C. by Arthure's hand
   D. in shame
   E. an unknown

9. Merlin predicts Arthure will experience a death that is:
   A. worshipful
   B. unattended
   C. dishonorable
   D. alone
   E. quick

10. At first Arthure disbelieves that Merlin knows:
    A. his parents
    B. his deeds
    C. the future
    D. how he will die
    E. his identity

WILLIAM SHAKESPEARE — HENRY V (1599)

SCENE III. The English camp.

Enter GLOUCESTER, BEDFORD, EXETER, ERPINGHAM, with all his host: SALISBURY and WESTMORELAND

5 GLOUCESTER Where is the king?

BEDFORD The king himself is rode to view their battle.

WESTMORELAND Of fighting men they have full three score thousand.

10 EXETER There's five to one; besides, they all are fresh.

SALISBURY God's arm strike with us! 'tis a fearful odds.
God be wi' you, princes all; I'll to my charge:
15 If we no more meet till we meet in heaven,
Then, joyfully, my noble Lord of Bedford,
My dear Lord Gloucester, and my good Lord Exeter,
And my kind kinsman, warriors all, adieu!

20 BEDFORD Farewell, good Salisbury; and good luck go with thee!

EXETER Farewell, kind lord; fight valiantly to-day:
And yet I do thee wrong to mind thee of it,
25 For thou art framed of the firm truth of valour.

Exit SALISBURY

BEDFORD He is full of valour as of kindness;
Princely in both.

Enter the KING

30 WESTMORELAND O that we now had here
But one ten thousand of those men in England
That do no work to-day!

KING HENRY V What's he that wishes so?
My cousin Westmoreland? No, my fair cousin:
35 If we are mark'd to die, we are enow
To do our country loss; and if to live,
The fewer men, the greater share of honour.
God's will! I pray thee, wish not one man more.
By Jove, I am not covetous for gold,
40 Nor care I who doth feed upon my cost;
It yearns me not if men my garments wear;
Such outward things dwell not in my desires:
But if it be a sin to covet honour,
I am the most offending soul alive.
45 No, faith, my coz, wish not a man from Eng-

William Shakespeare – Henry V (1599)

land:
God's peace! I would not lose so great an honour
As one man more, methinks, would share from
50 me
For the best hope I have. O, do not wish one more!
Rather proclaim it, Westmoreland, through my host,
55 That he which hath no stomach to this fight,
Let him depart; his passport shall be made
And crowns for convoy put into his purse:
We would not die in that man's company
That fears his fellowship to die with us.
60 This day is called the feast of Crispian:
He that outlives this day, and comes safe home,
Will stand a tip-toe when the day is named,
And rouse him at the name of Crispian.
He that shall live this day, and see old age,
65 Will yearly on the vigil feast his neighbours,
And say 'To-morrow is Saint Crispian:'
Then will he strip his sleeve and show his scars.
And say 'These wounds I had on Crispin's day.'
70 Old men forget: yet all shall be forgot,
But he'll remember with advantages
What feats he did that day: then shall our names.
Familiar in his mouth as household words
75 Harry the king, Bedford and Exeter,
Warwick and Talbot, Salisbury and Gloucester,
Be in their flowing cups freshly remember'd.
This story shall the good man teach his son;
And Crispin Crispian shall ne'er go by,
80 From this day to the ending of the world,
But we in it shall be remember'd;
We few, we happy few, we band of brothers;
For he to-day that sheds his blood with me
Shall be my brother; be he ne'er so vile,
85 This day shall gentle his condition:
And gentlemen in England now a-bed
Shall think themselves accursed they were not here,
And hold their manhoods cheap whiles any
90 speaks
That fought with us upon Saint Crispin's day.

Re-enter SALISBURY

SALISBURY My sovereign lord, bestow yourself with speed:
95 The French are bravely in their battles set,
And will with all expedience charge on us.

KING HENRY V All things are ready, if our minds be so.

WESTMORELAND Perish the man whose
100 mind is backward now!

KING HENRY V Thou dost not wish more help from England, coz?

WESTMORELAND God's will! my liege, would you and I alone,
105 Without more help, could fight this royal battle!

KING HENRY V Why, now thou hast unwish'd five thousand men;
Which likes me better than to wish us one.
110 You know your places: God be with you all!

William Shakespeare – *Henry V (1599)*

Exercises

1. As the battle approaches the English are:
   A. outnumbered
   B. despairing of victory
   C. lacking leadership
   D. feeling abandoned
   E. blessed by a priest

2. Henry says what bothers him is:
   A. the battle odds
   B. deserters
   C. the lack of reinforcements
   D. lack of determination
   E. the human cost of honor

3. Henry's troops number about:
   A. 1,000
   B. 3,000
   C. 10,000
   D. 12,000
   E. 20,000

4. Henry lists the things he doesn't mind, but doesn't mention:
   A. losing his army
   B. giving out money
   C. having a smaller army
   D. sharing his lands
   E. fearful soldiers

5. In Henry's speech (line 44) he would be "most offending" for not:
   A. being generous
   B. being a man of peace
   C. sharing command
   D. having hope
   E. desiring honor

6. The word "crown" (line 57) refers to:
   A. money
   B. a headpiece
   C. clout
   D. honors
   E. shame

7. Henry cites Gloucester, Bedford, and Exeter to:
   A. refer to a band of brothers
   B. recall those who may die in battle
   C. criticize their towns for insufficient soldiers
   D. cite men with whom he has drunk together
   E. honor their family names

8. The appeal of Henry's speech can be taken as:
   A. patriotic to England
   B. moral against the French enemy
   C. familial in protection
   D. memorial for future historians
   E. rousing for gloried retelling

9. The king rejects reinforcements lest they:
   A. dilute his army's honor
   B. are untrained as soldiers
   C. are too few to turn the tide of battle
   D. be late to arrive
   E. also be doomed

10. The word "backward" (line 100) seems to mean:
    A. wanting to retreat
    B. feeling homesick
    C. unhorsed
    D. confused
    E. unhelmeted

Jonathan Swift - Gulliver's Travels (1726)

The Luggnaggians are a polite and generous people, and although they are not without some share of that pride which is peculiar to all eastern countries, yet they shew themselves courteous to strangers, especially such who are countenanced by the court. I had many acquaintances among persons of the best fashion, and being always attended by my interpreter, the conversation we had was not disagreeable.

One day, in much good company, I was asked by a person of quality, whether I had seen any of their struldbrugs, or immortals. I said I had not; and desired he would explain to me what he meant by such an appellation, applied to a mortal creature. He told me, that sometimes, though very rarely, a child happened to be born in a family with a red circular spot in the forehead, directly over the left eye-brow, which was an infallible mark that it should never die. The spot, as he described it, was about the compass of a silver three-pence, but in the course of time grew larger, and changed its colour; for at twelve years old it became green, so continued till five and twenty, then turned to a deep blue; at five and forty it grew coal black, and as large as an English shilling; but never admitted any farther alteration. He said these births were so rare, that he did not believe there could be above eleven hundred struldbrugs of both sexes in the whole kingdom, of which he computed about fifty in the metropolis, and, among the rest, a young girl born, about three years ago; that these productions were not peculiar to any family, but a mere effect of chance; and the children of the struldbrugs themselves were equally mortal with the rest of the people.

I freely own myself to have been struck with inexpressible delight upon hearing this account: and the person who gave it me happening to understand the Balnibarbian language, which I spoke very well, I could not forbear breaking out into expressions, perhaps a little too extravagant. I cried out as in a rapture: "Happy nation, where every child hath at least a chance of being immortal! Happy people, who enjoy so many living examples of ancient virtue, and have masters ready to instruct them in the wisdom of all former ages! But happiest beyond all comparison are those excellent struldbrugs, who, born exempt from that universal calamity of human nature, have their minds free and disengaged, without the weight and depression of spirits caused by the continual apprehension of death." I discovered my admiration that I had not observed any of these illustrious persons at court; the black spot on the forehead being so remarkable a distinction, that I could not have easily overlooked it; and it was impossible that his Majesty, a most judicious prince, should not provide himself with a good number of such wise and able councilors. Yet perhaps the virtue of those reverend sages was too strict for the corrupt and libertine manners of a court. And we often find by experience, that young men are too opinionative and volatile to be guided by the sober dictates of their seniors. However, since the king was pleased to allow me access to his royal person, I was resolved, upon the very first occasion, to deliver my opinion to him on this matter freely, and at large, by the help of my interpreter; and whether he would please to take my advice or no, yet in one thing I was determined, that, his Majesty having frequently offered me an establishment in this country, I would with great thankfulness accept the favour, and pass my life here in the conversation of those superior beings, the struldbrugs, if they would please to admit me.

The gentlemen to whom I addressed my discourse, because (as I have already observed) he spoke the language of Balnibarbi, said to me with a sort of a smile, which usually ariseth from pity to the ignorant, that he was glad of any occasion to keep me among them, and desired my permission to explain to the company what I had spoke. He did so, and they talked together for some time in their own language, whereof I understood not a syllable, neither could I observe by their countenances, what impression my discourse had made on them. After a short silence, the same person told me, that his friends and mine (so he thought fit to express himself) were very much pleased with the judicious remarks I had made on the great happiness and advantages of immortal life, and they were desirous to know in a particular manner, what scheme of living I should have formed to myself, if it had fallen to my lot to have been born a struldbrug.

I answered, it was easy to be eloquent on so copious and delightful a subject, especially to me, who have been often apt to amuse myself with visions of what I should do, if I were a king, a general, or a great lord: and, upon this very case, I had frequently run over the whole system how I should employ myself, and pass the time, if I were sure to live for ever.

That, if it had been my good fortune to come into the world a struldbrug, as soon as I could discover my own happiness, by understanding the difference between life and death, I would first resolve, by all arts and methods whatsoever, to procure myself riches. In the pursuit of which, by thrift and management, I might reasonably expect, in about two hundred years, to be the wealthiest man in the kingdom. In the second place, I would from my earliest youth apply myself to the study of arts and sciences, by which I should arrive in time to excel all others in learning. Lastly, I would carefully record every action and event of consequence that happened in the public, impartially draw the characters of the several successions of princes, and great ministers of state, with my own observations on every point. I would exactly set down the several changes in customs, language, fashions of dress, diet and diversions. By all which acquirements, I should be a living treasury of knowledge and wisdom, and certainly become the oracle of the nation.

I would never marry after threescore, but live in an hospitable manner, yet still on the saving side. I would entertain myself in forming and directing the minds of hopeful young men, by convincing them from my own remembrance, experience and observation, fortified by numerous examples, of the usefulness of virtue in public and private life. But my choice and constant companions should be a set of my own immortal brotherhood, among whom I would elect a dozen from the most ancient, down to my own contemporaries. Where any of these wanted fortunes, I would provide them with convenient lodges round my own estate, and have some of them always at my table, only mingling a few of the most valuable among you mortals, whom length of time would harden me to lose, with little or no reluctance, and treat your posterity after the same manner; just as a man diverts himself with the annual succession of pinks and tulips in his garden, without regretting the loss of those which withered the preceding year.

These struldbrugs and I would mutually communicate our observations and memorials through the course of time; remark the several gradations by which corruption steals into the world, and oppose it in every step, by giving perpetual warning and instruction to mankind; which, added to the strong influence of our own example, would probably prevent that continual degeneracy of human nature, so justly complained of in all ages.

Add to all this, the pleasure of seeing the various revolutions of states and empires; the changes in the lower and upper world; ancient cities in ruins, and obscure villages become the seats of kings; famous rivers lessening into shallow brooks; the ocean leaving one coast dry, and overwhelming another; the discovery of many countries yet unknown; barbarity over-running the politest nations, and the most barbarous become civilized. I should then see the discovery of the longitude, the perpetual motion, the universal medicine, and many other great inventions brought to the utmost perfection.

What wonderful discoveries should we make in astronomy, by out-living and confirming our own predictions, by observing the progress and return of comets, with the changes of motion in the sun, moon, and stars.

I enlarged upon many other topics, which the natural desire of endless life and sublunary happiness could easily furnish me with. When I had ended, and the sum of my discourse had been interpreted, as before, to the rest of the company, there was a good deal of talk among them in the language of the country, not without some laughter at my expense. At last, the same gentleman who had been my interpreter said he was desired by the rest to set me right in a few mistakes, which I had fallen into through the common imbecility of human nature, and, upon that allowance, was less answerable for them. That this breed of struldbrugs was peculiar to their country, for there were no such people, either in Balnibarbi or Japan, where he had the honour to be ambassador from his Majesty, and found the natives in both those kingdoms very hard to believe that the fact was possible; and it appeared from my astonishment, when he first mentioned the matter to me, that I received it as a thing wholly new, and scarcely to be credited. That in the two kingdoms above mentioned, where, during his residence, he had conversed very much, he observed long life to be the universal desire and wish of mankind. That whoever had one foot in the grave, was sure to hold back the other as strongly as he could. That the oldest had still hopes of living one day longer, and looked on death as the greatest evil, from which Nature always prompted him to retreat; only in this island of Luggnagg the appetite for living was not so eager, from the continual example of the struldbrugs before their eyes.

That the system of living, contrived by me, was unreasonable and unjust, because it supposed a perpetuity of youth, health, and vigour, which no man could be so foolish to hope, however extravagant he may be in his wishes. That the question therefore was not whether a man would choose to be always in the prime of youth, attended with prosperity and health; but how he would pass a perpetual life under all the usual disadvantages which old age brings along with it. For although few men will avow their desires of being immortal upon such hard conditions, yet in the two kingdoms before mentioned, of Balnibarbi and Japan he observed that every man desired to put off death for some time longer, let it approach ever so late; and he rarely heard of any man who died willingly, except he were incited by the extremity of grief or torture. And he appealed to me, whether in those countries I had travelled, as well as my own, I had not observed the same general disposition.

After this preface, he gave me a particular account of the struldbrugs among them. He said they commonly acted like mortals, till about thirty years old, after which, by degrees, they grew melancholy and dejected, increasing in both till they came to fourscore. This he learned from their own confession; for otherwise, there not being above two or three of that species born in an age, they were too few to form a general observation by. When they came to fourscore years, which is reckoned the extremity of living in this country, they had not only all the follies and infirmities of other old men, but many more, which arose from the dreadful prospects of never dying. They were not only opinionative, peevish, covetous, morose, vain, talkative; but incapable of friendship, and dead to all natural affection, which never descended below their grandchildren. Envy and impotent desires are their prevailing passions. But those objects, against which their envy seems principally directed, are the vices of the younger sort, and the deaths of the old. By reflecting on the former, they find themselves cut off from all possibility of pleasure; and whenever they see a funeral, they lament and repine that others are gone to an harbour of rest, to which they themselves never can hope to arrive. They have no remembrance of anything but what they learned and observed in their youth and middle age, and even that is very imperfect. And, for the truth or particulars of any fact, it is safer to depend on common traditions, than upon their best recollections. The least miserable among them appear to be those who turn to dotage, and entirely lose their memories; these meet with more pity and assistance, because they want many bad qualities, which abound in others.

If a struldbrug happen to marry one of his own kind, the marriage is dissolved of course, by the courtesy of the kingdom, as soon as the younger of the two comes to be fourscore. For the law thinks it reasonable indulgence, that those who are condemned, without any fault of their own, to a perpetual continuance in the world, should not have their misery doubled by the load of a wife.

As soon as they have completed the term of eighty years, they are looked on as dead in law; their heirs immediately succeed to their estates, only a small pittance is reserved for their support; and the poor ones are maintained at the public charge. After that period they are held incapable of any employment of trust or profit, they cannot purchase lands, or take leases, neither are they allowed to be witnesses in any cause, either civil or criminal, not even for the decision of meers and bounds.

At ninety they lose their teeth and hair; they have at that age no distinction of taste, but eat and drink whatever they can get, without relish or appetite. The diseases they were subject to still continue, without increasing or diminishing. In talking, they forget the common appellation of things, and the names of persons, even of those who are their nearest friends and relations. For the same reason they never can amuse themselves with reading, because their memory will not serve to carry them from the beginning of a sentence to the end; and, by this defect, they are deprived of the only entertainment whereof they might otherwise be capable.

The language of this country being always upon the flux, the struldbrugs of one age do not understand those of another; neither are they able, after two hundred years, to hold any conversation (farther than by a few general words) with their neighbours, the mortals; and thus they lie under the disadvantage of living like foreigners in their own country.

This was the account given me of the struldbrugs, as near as I can remember. I afterwards saw five or six of different ages, the youngest not above two hundred years old, who were brought to me at several times, by some of my friends; but although they were told that I was a great traveller, and had seen all the world, they had not the least curiosity to ask me a question; only desired I would give them *slumskudask*, or a token of remembrance; which is a modest way of begging, to avoid the law that strictly forbids it, because they are provided for by the public, although, indeed, with a very scanty allowance.

They are despised and hated by all sorts of people; when one of them is born, it is reckoned ominous, and their birth is recorded very particularly; so that you may know their age, by consulting the register; which, however, hath not been kept above a thousand years past, or, at least, hath been destroyed by time, or public disturbances. But the usual way of computing how old they are, is, by asking them what kings or great persons they can remember, and then consulting history; for, infallibly, the last prince in their mind did not begin his reign after they were fourscore years old.

They were the most mortifying sight I ever beheld; and the women more horrible than the men. Besides the usual deformities in extreme old age, they acquired an additional ghastliness, in proportion to their number of years, which is not to be described; and, among half a dozen, I soon distinguished which was the eldest, although there was not above a century or two between them.

The reader will easily believe that from what I had heard and seen, my keen appetite for perpetuity of life was much abated. I grew heartily ashamed of the pleasing visions I had formed; and thought no tyrant could invent a death into which I would not run with pleasure from such a life. The king heard of all that had passed between me and my friends upon this occasion, and rallied me very pleasantly; wishing I would send a couple of struldbrugs to my own country, to arm our people against the fear of death; but this, it seems, is forbidden by the fundamental laws of the kingdom, or else I should have been well content with the trouble and expense of transporting them.

I could not but agree that the laws of this kingdom, relative to the struldbrugs, were founded upon the strongest reasons, and such as any other country would be under the necessity of enacting in the like circumstances. Otherwise, as avarice is the necessary consequent of old age, those immortals would in time become proprietors of the whole nation, and engross the civil power; which, for want of abilities to manage, must end in the ruin of the public.

Jonathan Swift - Gulliver's Travels (1726)

Exercises

1. The narrator's initial reaction to the report of the struldbrugs' existence is:
   A. disbelief
   B. shock
   C. delight
   D. questioning
   E. curiosity

2. The narrator seeks from the Luggnaggian king:
   A. an interpreter
   B. permission to speak
   C. a position as advisor
   D. a meeting with a struldbrug
   E. permission to live there

3. The narrator conjectures that the struldbrugs must be:
   A. wise
   B. fearless
   C. multi-lingual
   D. from special parents
   E. opinionated

4. Were he a struldbrug, the narrator says he would do all of the following except:
   A. become a historian
   B. never marry
   C. get rich
   D. become a scholar
   E. become a teacher

5. A spot on the forehead of some struldbrugs is at first:
   A. black
   B. red
   C. blue
   D. green
   E. invisible

6. The narrator says the universal calamity of human nature is:
   A. unhappiness
   B. lack of wisdom
   C. narrow-mindedness
   D. fear of death
   E. immorality

7. Mutual struldbrug marriages are terminated so that the struldbrugs:
   A. do not increase in number
   B. eventually will die out
   C. are happier
   D. are dispersed in the population
   E. don't concentrate their power

8. Aged struldbrugs are subject to all of following losses except:
   A. legal rights
   B. communication
   C. property
   D. longevity
   E. appetite

9. After strudbergs are 200 years old, which of the following is true?
   A. they can no longer move
   B. they can't hold a conversation
   C. they start to lose their teeth
   D. they lose their allowance
   E. they are reborn

10. The central idea dealt with in this passage is:
    A. satire
    B. accepting human differences
    C. Gulliver's adventurousness
    D. tolerance
    E. human frailty

CHARLES DICKENS – A TALE OF TWO CITIES (1859)

Chapter I - Recalled to Life

The Period

It was the best of times, it was the worst of times, it was the age of wisdom, it was the age of foolishness, it was the epoch of belief, it was the epoch of incredulity, it was the season of Light, it was the season of Darkness, it was the spring of hope, it was the winter of despair, we had everything before us, we had nothing before us, we were all going direct to Heaven, we were all going direct the other way--in short, the period was so far like the present period, that some of its noisiest authorities insisted on its being received, for good or for evil, in the superlative degree of comparison only.

There were a king with a large jaw and a queen with a plain face, on the throne of England; there were a king with a large jaw and a queen with a fair face, on the throne of France. In both countries it was clearer than crystal to the lords of the State preserves of loaves and fishes, that things in general were settled for ever.

It was the year of Our Lord one thousand seven hundred and seventy-five. Spiritual revelations were conceded to England at that favoured period, as at this. Mrs. Southcott had recently attained her five-and-twentieth blessed birthday, of whom a prophetic private in the Life Guards had heralded the sublime appearance by announcing that arrangements were made for the swallowing up of London and Westminster. Even the Cock-lane ghost had been laid only a round dozen of years, after rapping out its messages, as the spirits of this very year last past (supernaturally deficient in originality) rapped out theirs. Mere messages in the earthly order of events had lately come to the English Crown and People, from a congress of British subjects in America: which, strange to relate, have proved more important to the human race than any communications yet received through any of the chickens of the Cock-lane brood.

France, less favored on the whole as to matters spiritual than her sister of the shield and trident, rolled with exceeding smoothness down hill, making paper money and spending it. Under the guidance of her Christian pastors, she entertained herself, besides, with such humane achievements as sentencing a youth to have his hands cut off, his tongue torn out with pincers, and his body burned alive, because he had not kneeled down in the rain to do honor to a dirty procession of monks which passed within his view, at a distance of some fifty or sixty yards. It is likely enough that, rooted in the woods of France and Norway, there were growing trees, when that sufferer was put to death, already marked by the Woodman, Fate, to come down and be sawn into boards, to make a certain movable framework with a sack and a knife in it, terrible in history. It is likely enough that in the rough outhouses of some tillers of the heavy lands adjacent to Paris, there were sheltered from the weather that very day, rude carts, bespattered with rustic mire, snuffed about by pigs, and roosted in by poultry, which the Farmer, Death, had already set apart to be his tumbrils of the Revolution. But that Woodman and that Farmer, though they work unceasingly, work silently, and no one heard them as they went about with muffled tread: the rather, forasmuch as to entertain any suspicion that they were awake, was to be atheistical and traitorous.

In England, there was scarcely an amount of order and protection to justify much national boasting. Daring burglaries by armed men, and highway robberies, took place in the capital itself every night; families were publicly cautioned not to go out of town without removing their furniture to upholsterers' warehouses for security; the highwayman in the dark was a City tradesman in the light, and, being recognized and challenged by his fellow-tradesman whom he stopped in his character of "the Captain," gallantly shot him through the head and rode away; the mall was waylaid by seven robbers, and the guard shot three dead, and then got shot dead himself by the other four, "in consequence of the failure of his ammunition:" after which the mall was robbed in peace; that magnificent potentate, the Lord Mayor of London, was made to stand and deliver on Turnham Green, by one highwayman, who despoiled the illustrious creature in sight of all his retinue; prisoners in London gaols fought battles with their turnkeys, and the majesty of the law fired blunderbusses in among them, loaded with rounds of shot and ball; thieves snipped off diamond crosses from the necks of noble lords at Court drawing-rooms; musketeers went into St. Giles's, to search for contraband goods, and the mob fired on the musketeers, and the musketeers fired on the mob, and nobody thought any of these occurrences much out of the common way. In the midst of them, the hangman, ever busy and ever worse than useless, was in constant requisition; now, stringing up long rows of miscellaneous criminals; now, hanging a housebreaker on Saturday who had been taken on Tuesday; now, burning people in the hand at Newgate by the dozen, and now burning pamphlets at the door of Westminster Hall; to-day, taking the life of an atrocious murderer, and to-morrow of a wretched pilferer who had robbed a farmer's boy of sixpence.

All these things, and a thousand like them, came to pass in and close upon the dear old year one thousand seven hundred and seventy-five. Environed by them, while the Woodman and the Farmer worked unheeded, those two of the large jaws, and those other two of the plain and the fair faces, trod with stir enough, and carried their divine rights with a high hand. Thus did the year one thousand seven hundred and seventy-five conduct their Greatnesses, and

Charles Dickens – A Tale of Two Cities (1859)

myriads of small creatures--the creatures of this chronicle among the rest--along the roads that lay before them.

Exercises

1. In the opening lines, Dickens is mildly mocking:
   A. his current times
   B. religious believers
   C. human morality
   D. historians
   E. grammarians

2. In paragraph 2 Dickens is making fun of all of the following except:
   A. monarchy comparisons
   B. religion
   C. French monarchs
   D. English monarchs
   E. governments

3. In paragraph 3 a most "important" message relates to:
   A. spiritual life
   B. a birthday
   C. the possible destruction of London
   D. a ghost and chickens
   E. an English colony

4. In paragraph 4 in France a youth was burned to death for not kneeling to:
   A. the king
   B. the queen
   C. monks
   D. the prime minister
   E. parents

5. The term "tumbril" in line 76 means a:
   A. somersault
   B. drum
   C. reed instrument
   D. vehicle
   E. trumpet

6. The passage takes place in:
   A. 1775
   B. 1783
   C. 1789
   D. 1812
   E. can't be determined

7. The overall tone of the passage is:
   A. heroic
   B. cynical
   C. amused
   D. angry
   E. comical

8. The "mere messages" (line 41) refer most likely to:
   A. Revolutionary unrest
   B. supernatural signs
   C. hints of a plague
   D. war with France
   E. secret communications

9. Threats to France mentioned include:
   A. atheism
   B. inflation
   C. violent injustice
   D. growing rebellion
   E. outgrowth of plague

10. The next to last paragraph describes England's:
    A. class system
    B. superiority
    C. militarism
    D. war preparations
    E. crime

LEWIS CARROLL - THROUGH THE LOOKING GLASS (1871)

HUMPTY DUMPTY

However, the egg only got larger and larger, and more and more human: when she had come within a few yards of it, she saw
5 that it had eyes and a nose and mouth; and, when she had come close to it, she saw clearly that it was HUMPTY DUMPTY himself. `It can't be anybody else!' she said to herself. `I'm as certain of it, as if his
10 name were written all over his face!'

It might have been written a hundred times, easily, on that enormous face. Humpty Dumpty was sitting, with his legs crossed like a Turk, on the top of a high wall --
15 such a narrow one that Alice quite wondered how he could keep his balance -- and, as his eyes were steadily fixed in the opposite direction, and he didn't take the least notice of her, she thought he must be a
20 stuffed figure, after all.

`And how exactly like an egg he is!' she said aloud, standing with her hands ready to catch him, for she was every moment expecting him to fall.

25 `It's *very* provoking,' Humpty Dumpty said after a long silence, looking away from Alice as he spoke, `to be called an egg -- *very*!'

`I said you *looked* like an egg, Sir,' Alice gently explained. `And some eggs are very pretty, you
30 know,' she added, hoping to turn her remark into a sort of compliment.

`Some people,' said Humpty Dumpty, looking away from her as usual, `have no more sense than a baby!'

35 Alice didn't know what to say to this: it wasn't at all like conversation, she thought, as he never said anything to *her*; in fact, his last remark was evidently addressed to a tree -- so she stood and softly repeated to herself:

40 `*Humpty Dumpty sat on a wall:*
Humpty Dumpty had a great fall.
All the King's horses and all the King's men
Couldn't put Humpty Dumpty in his place
again.'

'That last line is much too long for the poetry,' she added, almost out loud, forgetting that Humpty Dumpty would hear her.

'Don't stand chattering to yourself like that,' Humpty Dumpty said, looking at her for the first time, 'but tell me your name and your business.'

'My *name* is Alice, but --'

'It's a stupid name enough!' Humpty Dumpty interrupted impatiently. 'What does it mean?'

'*Must* a name mean something?' Alice asked doubtfully.

'Of course it must,' Humpty Dumpty said with a short laugh: '*my* name means the shape I am -- and a good handsome shape it is, too. With a name like yours, you might be any shape, almost.'

'Why do you sit out here all alone?' said Alice, not wishing to begin an argument.

'Why, because there's nobody with me!' cried Humpty Dumpty. 'Did you think I didn't know the answer to *that*? Ask another.'

'Don't you think you'd be safer down on the ground?' Alice went on, not with any idea of making another riddle, but simply in her good-natured anxiety for the queer creature. 'That wall is so *very* narrow!'

'What tremendously easy riddles you ask!' Humpty Dumpty growled out. 'Of course I don't think so! Why, if ever I *did* fall off -- which there's no chance of -- but *if* I did --' Here he pursed up his lips, and looked so solemn and grand that Alice could hardly help laughing. '*If* I *did* fall,' he went on, '*the King has promised me* -- ah, you may turn pale, if you like! You didn't think I was going to say that, did you? *The King has promised me -- with his very own mouth* -- to -- to --'

'To send all his horses and all his men,' Alice interrupted, rather unwisely.

'Now I declare that's too bad!' Humpty Dumpty cried, breaking into a sudden passion. 'You've been listening at doors -- and behind trees -- and down chimneys -- or you couldn't have known it!'

'I haven't indeed!' Alice said very gently. 'It's in a book.'

'Ah, well! They may write such things in a *book*,' Humpty Dumpty said in a calmer tone. 'That's what you call a History of England, that is. Now, take a good look at me! I'm one that has spoken to a King, *I* am: mayhap you'll never see such another: and, to show you I'm not proud, you may shake hands with me!' And he grinned almost from ear to ear, as he leant forwards (and as nearly as possible fell off the wall in doing so) and offered Alice his hand. She watched him a little anxiously as she took it. 'If he smiled much more the ends of his mouth might meet behind,' she thought: 'And then I don't know *what* would happen to his head! I'm afraid it would come off!'

'Yes, all his horses and all his men,' Humpty Dumpty went on. 'They'd pick me up again in a minute, *they* would! However, this conversation is going on a little too fast: let's go back to the last remark but one.'

'I'm afraid I can't quite remember it,' Alice said, very politely.

'In that case we start afresh,' said Humpty Dumpty, 'and it's my turn to choose a subject --' ('He talks about it just as if it was a game!' thought Alice.) 'So here's a question for you. How old did you say you were?'

Alice made a short calculation, and said 'Seven years and six months.'

'Wrong!' Humpty Dumpty exclaimed triumphantly. 'You never said a word like it!'

'I thought you meant "How old *are* you?"' Alice explained.

'If I'd meant that, I'd have said it,' said Humpty Dumpty.

Alice didn't want to begin another argument, so she said nothing.

'Seven years and six months!' Humpty Dumpty repeated thoughtfully. 'An uncomfortable sort of age. Now if you'd asked *my* advice, I'd have said "Leave off at seven" -- but it's too late now.'

'I never ask advice about growing,' Alice said indignantly.

'Too proud?' the other enquired.

Alice felt even more indignant at this suggestion. 'I mean,' she said, 'that one can't help growing older.'

'*One* can't, perhaps,' said Humpty Dumpty; 'but *two* can. With proper assistance, you might have left off at seven.'

'What a beautiful belt you've got on!' Alice suddenly remarked. (They had had quite enough of the subject of age, she thought: and, if they really were to take turns in choosing subjects, it was *her* turn now.) 'At least,' she corrected herself on second thoughts, 'a beautiful cravat, I should have said -- no, a belt, I mean -- I beg your pardon!' she added in dismay, for Humpty Dumpty looked thoroughly offended, and she began to wish she hadn't chosen that subject. 'If only I knew,' she thought to herself, 'which was neck and which was waist!'

Evidently Humpty Dumpty was very angry, though he said nothing for a minute or two. When he *did* speak again, it was in a deep growl.

'It is a -- *most* -- *provoking* -- thing,' he said at last, 'when a person doesn't know a cravat from a belt!'

'I know it's very ignorant of me,' Alice said, in so humble a tone that Humpty Dumpty relented.

'It's a cravat, child, and a beautiful one, as you say. It's a present from the White King and Queen. There now!'

'Is it really?' said Alice, quite pleased to find that she *had* chosen a good subject after all.

'They gave it me,' Humpty Dumpty continued thoughtfully as he crossed one knee over the other and clasped his hands round it, 'they gave it me -- for an un-birthday present.'

'I beg your pardon?' Alice said with a puzzled air.

'I'm not offended,' said Humpty Dumpty.

'I mean, what *is* an un-birthday present?'

'A present given when it isn't your birthday, of course.'

Alice considered a little. 'I like birthday presents best,' she said at last.

'You don't know what you're talking about!' cried Humpty Dumpty. 'How many days are there in a year?'

'Three hundred and sixty-five,' said Alice.

'And how many birthdays have you?'

'One.'

'And if you take one from three hundred and sixty-five what remains?'

'Three hundred and sixty-four, of course.'

Humpty Dumpty looked doubtful. 'I'd rather see that done on paper,' he said.

Alice couldn't help smiling as she took out her memorandum book, and worked the sum for him:

```
 365
  -1
----
 364
----
```

Humpty Dumpty took the book and looked at it carefully. 'That seems to be done right --' he began.

'You're holding it upside down!' Alice interrupted.

'To be sure I was!' Humpty Dumpty said gaily as she turned it round for him. 'I thought it looked a little queer. As I was saying, that *seems* to be done right -- though I haven't time to look it over thoroughly just now -- and that shows that there are three hundred and sixty-four days when you might get un-birthday presents --'

'Certainly,' said Alice.

'And only *one* for birthday presents, you know. There's glory for you!'

220 'I don't know what you mean by "glory",' Alice said.

Humpty Dumpty smiled contemptuously. 'Of course you don't -- till I tell you. I meant "there's a nice knock-down argument
225 for you!"'

'But "glory" doesn't mean "a nice knock-down argument",' Alice objected.

'When *I* use a word,' Humpty Dumpty said, in rather a scornful tone, 'it means just what I
230 choose it to mean -- neither more nor less.'

'The question is,' said Alice, 'whether you *can* make words mean so many different things.'

'The question is,' said Humpty Dumpty, 'which is to be master -- that's all.'

235 Alice was too much puzzled to say anything; so after a minute Humpty Dumpty began again. 'They've a temper, some of them -- particularly verbs: they're the proudest -- adjectives you can do anything with, but not verbs -- however,
240 *I* can manage the whole lot of them! Impenetrability! That's what *I* say!'

'Would you tell me please,' said Alice, 'what that means?'

'Now you talk like a reasonable child,' said
245 Humpty Dumpty, looking very much pleased. 'I meant by "impenetrability" that we've had enough of that subject, and it would be just as well if you'd mention what you mean to do next, as I suppose you don't
250 mean to stop here all the rest of your life.'

'That's a great deal to make one word mean,' Alice said in a thoughtful tone.

'When I make a word do a lot of work like that,' said Humpty Dumpty, 'I always pay it
255 extra.'

'Oh!' said Alice. She was too much puzzled to make any other remark.

'Ah, you should see 'em come round me of a Saturday night,' Humpty Dumpty went
260 on, wagging his head gravely from side to side, 'for to get their wages, you know.'

(Alice didn't venture to ask what he paid them with; and so you see I can't tell *you*.)

'You seem very clever at explaining words,
265 Sir,' said Alice. 'Would you kindly tell me the meaning of the poem called "Jabberwocky"?'

'Let's hear it,' said Humpty Dumpty. 'I can explain all the poems that ever were invent-
270 ed -- and a good many that haven't been invented just yet.'

This sounded very hopeful, so Alice repeated the first verse:

'*'Twas brillig, and the slithy toves
275 Did gyre and gimble in the wabe:
All mimsy were the borogoves,
And the mome raths outgrabe.*'

'That's enough to begin with,' Humpty Dumpty interrupted: 'there are plenty of hard words
280 there. "*Brillig*" means four o'clock in the afternoon -- the time when you begin *broiling* things for dinner.'

'That'll do very well,' said Alice: 'and "*slithy*"?'

'Well, "*slithy*" means "lithe and slimy". "Lithe"
285 is the same as "active". You see it's like a portmanteau -- there are two meanings packed up into one word.'

'I see it now,' Alice remarked thoughtfully: 'and what are "*toves*"?'

290 'Well, "*toves*" are something like badgers -- they're something like lizards -- and they're something like corkscrews.'

'They must be very curious-looking creatures.'

295 'They are that,' said Humpty Dumpty; 'also they make their nests under sun-dials -- also they live on cheese.'

'And what's to "*gyre*" and to "*gimble*"?'

'To "*gyre*" is to go round and round like a gyroscope. To "*gimble*" is to make holes like a gimlet.'

'And "*the wabe*" is the grass-plot round a sundial, I suppose?' said Alice, surprised at her own ingenuity.

'Of course it is. It's called "*wabe*" you know, because it goes a long way before it, and a long way behind it --'

'And a long way beyond it on each side,' Alice added.

'Exactly so. Well then, "mimsy" is "flimsy and miserable" (there's another portmanteau for you). And a "borogove" is a thin shabby-looking bird with its feathers sticking out all round -- something like a live mop.'

'And then "*mome raths*"?' said Alice. 'I'm afraid I'm giving you a great deal of trouble.'

'Well, a "*rath*" is a sort of green pig: but "*mome*" I'm not certain about. I think it's short for "from home" -- meaning that they'd lost their way, you know.'

'And what does "*outgrabe*" mean?'

'Well, "*outgribing*" is something between bellowing and whistling, with a kind of sneeze in the middle: however, you'll hear it done, maybe -- down in the wood yonder -- and, when you've once heard it, you'll be *quite* content. Who's been repeating all that hard stuff to you?'

'I read it in a book,' said Alice. 'But I *had* some poetry repeated to me much easier than that, by -- Tweedledee, I think.'

'As to poetry, you know,' said Humpty Dumpty, stretching out one of his great hands, '*I* can repeat poetry as well as other folk, if it comes to that --'

'Oh, it needn't come to that!' Alice hastily said, hoping to keep him from beginning.

'The piece I'm going to repeat,' he went on without noticing her remark, 'was written entirely for your amusement.'

Alice felt that in that case she really *ought* to listen to it; so she sat down, and said 'Thank you' rather sadly,

In winter, when the fields are white,
I sing this song for your delight --

only I don't sing it,' he added, as an explanation.

'I see you don't,' said Alice.

'If you can *see* whether I'm singing or not, you've sharper eyes than most,' Humpty Dumpty remarked severely. Alice was silent.

In spring, when woods are getting green,
I'll try and tell you what I mean:

'Thank you very much,' said Alice.

In summer, when the days are long,
Perhaps you'll understand the song:

In autumn, when the leaves are brown,
Take pen and ink, and write it down.'

'I will, if I can remember it so long,' said Alice.

'You needn't go on making remarks like that,' Humpty Dumpty said: 'they're not sensible, and they put me out.'

I sent a message to the fish:
I told them "This is what I wish."

The little fishes of the sea,
They sent an answer back to me.

The little fishes' answer was
"We cannot do it, Sir, because --"'

'I'm afraid I don't quite understand,' said Alice.

'It gets easier further on,' Humpty Dumpty replied.

I sent to them again to say
"It will be better to obey."

The fishes answered, with a grin,
"Why, what a temper you are in!"

I told them once, I told them twice:
They would not listen to advice.

*I took a kettle large and new,
Fit for the deed I had to do.*

*My heart went hop, my heart went thump:
I filled the kettle at the pump.*

*Then some one came to me and said
"The little fishes are in bed."*

*I said to him, I said it plain,
"Then you must wake them up again."*

*I said it very loud and clear:
I went and shouted in his ear.'*

Humpty Dumpty raised his voice almost to a scream as he repeated this verse, and Alice thought with a shudder, `I wouldn't have been the messenger for *anything*!'

*`But he was very stiff and proud:
He said, "You needn't shout so loud!"*

*And he was very proud and stiff:
He said "I'd go and wake them, if--"*

*I took a corkscrew from the shelf:
I went to wake them up myself.*

*And when I found the door was locked,
I pulled and pushed and kicked and knocked.*

*And when I found the door was shut,
I tried to turn the handle, but--'*

There was a long pause.

`Is that all?' Alice timidly asked.

`That's all,' said Humpty Dumpty. `Good-bye.'

This was rather sudden, Alice thought: but, after such a *very* strong hint that she ought to be going, she felt that it would hardly be civil to stay. So she got up, and held out her hand. `Good-bye, till we meet again!' she said as cheerfully as she could.

`I shouldn't know you again if we *did* meet,' Humpty Dumpty replied in a discontented tone, giving her one of his fingers to shake: `you're so exactly like other people.'

`The face is what one goes by, generally,' Alice remarked in a thoughtful tone.

`That's just what I complain of,' said Humpty Dumpty. `Your face is the same as everybody has -- the two eyes, so --' (marking their places in the air with his thumb) `nose in the middle, mouth under. It's always the same. Now if you had the two eyes on the same side of the nose, for instance -- or the mouth at the top -- that would be *some* help.'

`It wouldn't look nice,' Alice objected. But Humpty Dumpty only shut his eyes, and said `Wait till you've tried.'

Alice waited a minute to see if he would speak again, but, as he never opened his eyes or took any further notice of her, she said `Good-bye!' once more, and, getting no answer to this, she quietly walked away: but she couldn't help saying to herself, as she went, `of all the unsatisfactory --' (she repeated this aloud, as it was a great comfort to have such a long word to say) `of all the unsatisfactory people I *ever* met --' She never finished the sentence, for at this moment a heavy crash shook the forest from end to end.

Lewis Carroll - Through the Looking Glass (1871)

Exercises

1. This episode's primary focus is on:
   A. nursery rhymes
   B. poetry
   C. word meanings
   D. proper manners
   E. riddles

2. Humpty Dumpty objects to Alice's name because it:
   A. is shapeless
   B. sounds childish
   C. doesn't rhyme
   D. has no obvious meaning
   E. doesn't sound feminine

3. Saying: "The question is…which is to be master" (l. 234) Humpty Dumpty refers to:
   A. Alice's remarks versus his own
   B. the White King versus himself
   C. his chronic indecision
   D. the meaning of words
   E. grammar

4. Saying: "*I* can manage the whole lot of them" Humpty Dumpty implies:
   A. pronouns can control verbs
   B. he's an expert linguist
   C. words mean whatever he wants
   D. he can choose what he says
   E. he knows the parts of speech

5. The confusion between a cravat and a belt involves (line 144):
   A. Humpty Dumpty's being oddly dressed
   B. Alice's being unsure what a cravat is
   C. Alice not knowing a belt from a cravat
   D. Humpty Dumpty's odd body parts
   E. Humpty Dumpty's pride in a royal gift

6. Humpty Dumpty says he won't know Alice on a subsequent encounter because:
   A. people all look the same
   B. she'll be that much older
   C. he'll have forgotten this initial meeting
   D. her voice will have changed
   E. she'll likely be dressed differently

7. Alice repeats the word "unsatisfactory" because she is (line 437, 440):
   A. determined to save face as she departs
   B. upset with the abrupt end of their encounter
   C. sure Humpty Dumpty isn't listening
   D. anxious to communicate her displeasure
   E. proud of using a polysyllabic word

8. Humpty Dumpty objects to Alice's:
   A. name
   B. shape
   C. face
   D. feminine manners
   E. going off-topic

9. The Jabberwocky seems to Alice to be:
   A. a talkative clown
   B. a character from a book
   C. learned about in school
   D. told her by Tweedledum
   E. a menace

10. In this passage the author's main subject is:
    A. words
    B. conversation
    C. incompatibility
    D. arithmetic
    E. the calendar

H. G. Wells – The Time Machine – XII – (1895)

So I came back. For a long time I must have been insensible upon the machine. The blinking succession of the days and nights was resumed, the sun got golden again, the sky blue. I breathed with greater freedom. The fluctuating contours of the land ebbed and flowed. The hands spun backward upon the dials. At last I saw again the dim shadows of houses, the evidences of decadent humanity. These, too, changed and passed, and others came. Presently, when the million dial was at zero, I slackened speed. I began to recognize our own petty and familiar architecture, the thousands hand ran back to the starting-point, the night and day flapped slower and slower. Then the old walls of the laboratory came round me. Very gently, now, I slowed the mechanism down.

`I saw one little thing that seemed odd to me. I think I have told you that when I set out, before my velocity became very high, Mrs. Watchett had walked across the room, traveling, as it seemed to me, like a rocket. As I returned, I passed again across that minute when she traversed the laboratory. But now her every motion appeared to be the exact inversion of her previous ones. The door at the lower end opened, and she glided quietly up the laboratory, back foremost, and disappeared behind the door by which she had previously entered. Just before that I seemed to see Hillyer for a moment; but he passed like a flash.

`Then I stopped the machine, and saw about me again the old familiar laboratory, my tools, my appliances just as I had left them. I got off the thing very shaky, and sat down upon my bench. For several minutes I trembled violently. Then I became calmer. Around me was my old workshop again, exactly as it had been. I might have slept there, and the whole thing have been a dream

`And yet, not exactly! The thing had started from the south-east corner of the laboratory. It had come to rest again in the north-west, against the wall where you saw it. That gives you the exact distance from my little lawn to the pedestal of the White Sphinx, into which the Morlocks had carried my machine.

'For a time my brain went stagnant. Presently I got up and came through the passage here, limping, because my heel was still painful, and feeling sorely begrimed. I saw the PALL MALL GAZETTE on the table by the door. I found the date was indeed today, and looking at the timepiece, saw the hour was almost eight o'clock. I heard your voices and the clatter of plates. I hesitated--I felt so sick and weak. Then I sniffed good wholesome meat, and opened the door on you. You know the rest. I washed, and dined, and now I am telling you the story.

'I know,' he said, after a pause, 'that all this will be absolutely incredible to you. To me the one incredible thing is that I am here to-night in this old familiar room looking into your friendly faces and telling you these strange adventures.'

He looked at the Medical Man. 'No. I cannot expect you to believe it. Take it as a lie--or a prophecy. Say I dreamed it in the workshop. Consider I have been speculating upon the destinies of our race until I have hatched this fiction. Treat my assertion of its truth as a mere stroke of art to enhance its interest. And taking it as a story, what do you think of it?'

He took up his pipe, and began, in his old accustomed manner, to tap with it nervously upon the bars of the grate. There was a momentary stillness. Then chairs began to creak and shoes to scrape upon the carpet. I took my eyes off the Time Traveler's face, and looked round at his audience. They were in the dark, and little spots of color swam before them. The Medical Man seemed absorbed in the contemplation of our host. The Editor was looking hard at the end of his cigar--the sixth. The Journalist fumbled for his watch. The others, as far as I remember, were motionless.

The Editor stood up with a sigh. 'What a pity it is you're not a writer of stories!' he said, putting his hand on the Time Traveler's shoulder.

'You don't believe it?'

'Well----'

'I thought not.'

The Time Traveler turned to us. 'Where are the matches?' he said. He lit one and spoke over his pipe, puffing. 'To tell you the truth . . . I hardly believe it myself. . . . And yet . . .'

His eye fell with a mute inquiry upon the withered white flowers upon the little table. Then he turned over the hand holding his pipe, and I saw he was looking at some half-healed scars on his knuckles.

The Medical Man rose, came to the lamp, and examined the flowers. 'The gynaeceum's odd,' he said. The Psychologist leant forward to see, holding out his hand for a specimen.

'I'm hanged if it isn't a quarter to one,' said the Journalist. 'How shall we get home?'

'Plenty of cabs at the station,' said the Psychologist.

'It's a curious thing,' said the Medical Man; 'but I certainly don't know the natural order of these flowers. May I have them?'

The Time Traveler hesitated. Then suddenly: 'Certainly not.'

'Where did you really get them?' said the Medical Man.

The Time Traveler put his hand to his head. He spoke like one who was trying to keep hold of an idea that eluded him.

'They were put into my pocket by Weena, when I traveled into Time.' He stared round the room. `I'm damned if it isn't all going. This room and you and the atmosphere of every day is too much for my memory. Did I ever make a Time Machine, or a model of a Time Machine? Or is it all only a dream? They say life is a dream, a precious poor dream at times--but I can't stand another that won't fit. It's madness. And where did the dream come from? . . . I must look at that machine. If there is one!'

He caught up the lamp swiftly, and carried it, flaring red, through the door into the corridor. We followed him. There in the flickering light of the lamp was the machine sure enough, squat, ugly, and askew; a thing of brass, ebony, ivory, and translucent glimmering quartz. Solid to the touch--for I put out my hand and felt the rail of it--and with brown spots and smears upon the ivory, and bits of grass and moss upon the lower parts, and one rail bent awry.

The Time Traveler put the lamp down on the bench, and ran his hand along the damaged rail. `It's all right now,' he said. 'The story I told you was true. I'm sorry to have brought you out here in the cold.' He took up the lamp, and, in an absolute silence, we returned to the smoking-room.

He came into the hall with us and helped the Editor on with his coat. The Medical Man looked into his face and, with a certain hesitation, told him he was suffering from overwork, at which he laughed hugely. I remember him standing in the open doorway, bawling good night.

I shared a cab with the Editor. He thought the tale a `gaudy lie.' For my own part I was unable to come to a conclusion. The story was so fantastic and incredible, the telling so credible and sober. I lay awake most of the night thinking about it. I determined to go next day and see the Time Traveler again. I was told he was in the laboratory, and being on easy terms in the house, I went up to him. The laboratory, however, was empty. I

stared for a minute at the Time Machine and put out my hand and touched the lever. At that the squat substantial-looking mass swayed like a bough shaken by the wind. Its instability startled me extremely, and I had a queer reminiscence of the childish days when I used to be forbidden to meddle. I came back through the corridor. The Time Traveler met me in the smoking-room. He was coming from the house. He had a small camera under one arm and a knapsack under the other. He laughed when he saw me, and gave me an elbow to shake. `I'm frightfully busy,' said he, `with that thing in there.'

`But is it not some hoax?' I said. `Do you really travel through time?'

`Really and truly I do.' And he looked frankly into my eyes. He hesitated. His eye wandered about the room. `I only want half an hour,' he said. `I know why you came, and it's awfully good of you. There's some magazines here. If you'll stop to lunch I'll prove you this time traveling up to the hilt, specimen and all. If you'll forgive my leaving you now?'

I consented, hardly comprehending then the full import of his words, and he nodded and went on down the corridor. I heard the door of the laboratory slam, seated myself in a chair, and took up a daily paper. What was he going to do before lunchtime? Then suddenly I was reminded by an advertisement that I had promised to meet Richardson, the publisher, at two. I looked at my watch, and saw that I could barely save that engagement. I got up and went down the passage to tell the Time Traveler.

As I took hold of the handle of the door I heard an exclamation, oddly truncated at the end, and a click and a thud. A gust of air whirled round me as I opened the door, and from within came the sound of broken glass falling on the floor. The Time Traveler was not there. I seemed to see a ghostly, indistinct figure sitting in a whirling mass of black and brass for a moment--a figure so transparent that the bench behind with its sheets of drawings was absolutely distinct; but this phantasm vanished as I rubbed my eyes. The Time Machine had gone. Save for a subsiding stir of dust, the further end of the laboratory was empty. A pane of the skylight had, apparently, just been blown in.

I felt an unreasonable amazement. I knew that something strange had happened, and for the moment could not distinguish what the strange thing might be. As I stood staring, the door into the garden opened, and the manservant appeared.

We looked at each other. Then ideas began to come. `Has Mr. ---- gone out that way?' said I.

`No, sir. No one has come out this way. I was expecting to find him here.'

At that I understood. At the risk of disappointing Richardson I stayed on, waiting for the Time Traveler; waiting for the second, perhaps still stranger story, and the specimens and photographs he would bring with him. But I am beginning now to fear that I must wait a lifetime. The Time Traveler vanished three years ago. And, as everybody knows now, he has never returned.

H. G. Wells – The Time Machine – XII – (1895)

Exercises

1. The genre or type of story this tale most nearly represents is:
   A. fantasy
   B. make-believe
   C. juvenile literature
   D. science fiction
   E. magic realism

2. The person relating this story is:
   A. the Medical Man
   B. an editor
   C. a psychologist
   D. the Time Traveler
   E. none of the above

3. The Time Traveler has apparently journeyed how many years into the future?
   A. over a million
   B. thousands
   C. hundreds
   D. scores
   E. fifty

4. The person who most believes the Time Traveler is:
   A. the Editor
   B. the Medical Man
   C. the Journalist
   D. the Psychologist
   E. the narrator

5. Physical evidence of the Time Traveler's claims includes all of the following except:
   A. scars on his hand
   B. a stopped watch
   C. bits of grass
   D. a dirty piece of ivory
   E. a bent rail

6. The *gynaeceum* (line 115) and surrounding dialogue hint that the Time Traveler is:
   A. highly possessive
   B. linguist
   C. a scientist
   D. in love
   E. absent-minded

7. At the end of the passage, one can surmise that the Time Traveler will:
   A. bring back photographic proof
   B. bring back specimens
   C. return in a short while
   D. not miss his comrades
   E. not return

8. The story takes place during:
   A. an evening
   B. over 24 hours
   C. the narrator's dream
   D. the future in England
   E. over a year

9. The Time Machine is described as:
   A. beautiful
   B. ingenious
   C. insubstantial
   D. unstable
   E. a figment of the narrator's imagination

10. The Time Traveler presumably returns to the future primarily to:
    A. battle the Morlocks
    B. bring back evidence of his journey
    C. be with Weena
    D. avert disaster
    E. impress his company

RUDYARD KIPLING – HOW THE LEOPARD GOT HIS SPOTS (1902)

In the days when everybody started fair, Best Beloved, the Leopard lived in a place called the High Veldt. 'Member it wasn't the Low Veldt, or the Bush Veldt, or the
5 Sour Veldt, but the 'sclusively bare, hot, shiny High Veldt, where there was sand and sandy-coloured rock and 'sclusively tufts of sandy- yellowish grass. The Giraffe and the Zebra and the Eland and the
10 Koodoo and the Hartebeest lived there; and they were 'sclusively sandy-yellow-brownish all over; but the Leopard, he was the 'sclusivest sandiest-yellowish-brownest of them all--a greyish-yellowish catty-shaped
15 kind of beast, and he matched the 'sclusively yellowish-greyish-brownish colour of the High Veldt to one hair. This was very bad for the Giraffe and the Zebra and the rest of them; for he would lie down by a 'sclusive-
20 ly yellowish-greyish-brownish stone or clump of grass, and when the Giraffe or the Zebra or the Eland or the Koodoo or the Bush-Buck or the Bonte-Buck came by he would surprise them out of their jumpsome
25 lives. He would indeed! And, also, there was an Ethiopian with bows and arrows (a 'sclusively greyish-brownish-yellowish man he was then), who lived on the High Veldt with the Leopard; and the two used to hunt
30 together--the Ethiopian with his bows and arrows, and the Leopard 'sclusively with his teeth and claws--till the Giraffe and the Eland and the Koodoo and the Quagga and all the rest of them didn't know which way
35 to jump, Best Beloved. They didn't indeed!

After a long time--things lived for ever so long in those days--they learned to avoid anything that looked like a Leopard or an Ethiopian; and bit by bit--the Giraffe began
40 it, because his legs were the longest--they went away from the High Veldt. They scuttled for days and days and days till they came to a great forest, 'sclusively full of trees and bushes and stripy, speckly,
45 patchy-blatchy shadows, and there they hid: and after another long time, what with standing half in the shade and half out of it, and what with the slippery-slidy shadows of the trees falling on them, the Giraffe

grew blotchy, and the Zebra grew stripy, and the Eland and the Koodoo grew darker, with little wavy grey lines on their backs like bark on a tree trunk; and so, though you could hear them and smell them, you could very seldom see them, and then only when you knew precisely where to look. They had a beautiful time in the 'sclusively speckly-spickly shadows of the forest, while the Leopard and the Ethiopian ran about over the 'sclusively greyish-yellowish-reddish High Veldt outside, wondering where all their breakfasts and their dinners and their teas had gone. At last they were so hungry that they ate rats and beetles and rock-rabbits, the Leopard and the Ethiopian, and then they had the Big Tummy-ache, both together; and then they met Baviaan-- the dog-headed, barking Baboon, who is Quite the Wisest Animal in All South Africa.

Said Leopard to Baviaan (and it was a very hot day), 'Where has all the game gone?'

And Baviaan winked. He knew.

Said the Ethiopian to Baviaan, 'Can you tell me the present habitat of the aboriginal Fauna?' (That meant just the same thing, but the Ethiopian always used long words. He was a grown-up.)

And Baviaan winked. He knew.

Then said Baviaan, 'The game has gone into other spots; and my advice to you, Leopard, is to go into other spots as soon as you can.'

And the Ethiopian said, 'That is all very fine, but I wish to know whither the aboriginal Fauna has migrated.'

Then said Baviaan, 'The aboriginal Fauna has joined the aboriginal Flora because it was high time for a change; and my advice to you, Ethiopian, is to change as soon as you can.'

That puzzled the Leopard and the Ethiopian, but they set off to look for the aboriginal Flora, and presently, after ever so many days, they saw a great, high, tall forest full of tree trunks all 'sclusively speckled and sprottled and spottled, dotted and splashed and slashed and hatched and cross-hatched with shadows. (Say that quickly aloud, and you will see how very shadowy the forest must have been.)

'What is this,' said the Leopard, 'that is so 'sclusively dark, and yet so full of little pieces of light?'

'I don't know, said the Ethiopian, 'but it ought to be the aboriginal Flora. I can smell Giraffe, and I can hear Giraffe, but I can't see Giraffe.'

'That's curious,' said the Leopard. 'I suppose it is because we have just come in out of the sunshine. I can smell Zebra, and I can hear Zebra, but I can't see Zebra.'

'Wait a bit, said the Ethiopian. 'It's a long time since we've hunted 'em. Perhaps we've forgotten what they were like.'

'Fiddle!' said the Leopard. 'I remember them perfectly on the High Veldt, especially their marrow-bones. Giraffe is about seventeen feet high, of a 'sclusively fulvous golden-yellow from head to heel; and Zebra is about four and a half feet high, of a 'sclusively grey-fawn colour from head to heel.'

'Umm, said the Ethiopian, looking into the speckly-spickly shadows of the aboriginal Flora-forest. 'Then they ought to show up in this dark place like ripe bananas in a smokehouse.'

But they didn't. The Leopard and the Ethiopian hunted all day; and though they could smell them and hear them, they never saw one of them.

'For goodness' sake,' said the Leopard at tea-time, 'let us wait till it gets dark. This daylight hunting is a perfect scandal.'

So they waited till dark, and then the Leopard heard something breathing sniffily in the starlight that fell all stripy through the branches, and he jumped at the noise, and it smelt like Zebra, and it felt like Zebra, and when he knocked it down it kicked like Zebra, but he couldn't see it. So he said, 'Be quiet, O you person without any form. I am going to sit on your head till morning, because there is something about you that I don't understand.'

Presently he heard a grunt and a crash and a scramble, and the Ethiopian called out, 'I've caught a thing that I can't see. It smells like Giraffe, and it kicks like Giraffe, but it hasn't any form.'

'Don't you trust it,' said the Leopard. 'Sit on its head till the morning--same as me. They haven't any form--any of 'em.'

So they sat down on them hard till bright morning-time, and then Leopard said, 'What have you at your end of the table, Brother?'

The Ethiopian scratched his head and said, 'It ought to be 'sclusively a rich fulvous orange-tawny from head to heel, and it ought to be Giraffe; but it is covered all over with chestnut blotches. What have you at your end of the table, Brother?'

And the Leopard scratched his head and said, 'It ought to be 'sclusively a delicate greyish-fawn, and it ought to be Zebra; but it is covered all over with black and purple stripes. What in the world have you been doing to yourself, Zebra? Don't you know that if you were on the High Veldt I could see you ten miles off? You haven't any form.'

'Yes,' said the Zebra, 'but this isn't the High Veldt. Can't you see?'

'I can now,' said the Leopard. 'But I couldn't all yesterday. How is it done?'

'Let us up,' said the Zebra, 'and we will show you.'

They let the Zebra and the Giraffe get up; and Zebra moved away to some little thorn-bushes where the sunlight fell all stripy, and Giraffe moved off to some tallish trees where the shadows fell all blotchy.

'Now watch,' said the Zebra and the Giraffe. 'This is the way it's done. One--two--three! And where's your breakfast?'

Leopard stared, and Ethiopian stared, but all they could see were stripy shadows and blotched shadows in the forest, but never a sign of Zebra and Giraffe. They had just walked off and hidden themselves in the shadowy forest.

'Hi! Hi!' said the Ethiopian. 'That's a trick worth learning. Take a lesson by it, Leopard. You show up in this dark place like a bar of soap in a coal-scuttle.'

'Ho! Ho!' said the Leopard. 'Would it surprise you very much to know that you show up in this dark place like a mustard-plaster on a sack of coals?'

'Well, calling names won't catch dinner, said the Ethiopian. 'The long and the little of it is that we don't match our backgrounds. I'm going to take Baviaan's advice. He told me I ought to change; and as I've nothing to change except my skin I'm going to change that.'

'What to?' said the Leopard, tremendously excited.

'To a nice working blackish-brownish colour, with a little purple in it, and touches of slaty-blue. It will be the very thing for hiding in hollows and behind trees.'

So he changed his skin then and there, and the Leopard was more excited than ever; he had never seen a man change his skin before.

'But what about me?' he said, when the Ethiopian had worked his last little finger into his fine new black skin.

'You take Baviaan's advice too. He told you to go into spots.'

'So I did,' said the Leopard. I went into other spots as fast as I could. I went into this spot with you, and a lot of good it has done me.'

'Oh,' said the Ethiopian, 'Baviaan didn't mean spots in South Africa. He meant spots on your skin.'

'What's the use of that?' said the Leopard.

'Think of Giraffe,' said the Ethiopian. 'Or if you prefer stripes, think of Zebra. They find their spots and stripes give them per-feet satisfaction.'

'Umm,' said the Leopard. 'I wouldn't look like Zebra--not for ever so.'

'Well, make up your mind,' said the Ethiopian, 'because I'd hate to go hunting without you, but I must if you insist on looking like a sun-flower against a tarred fence.'

'I'll take spots, then,' said the Leopard; 'but don't make 'em too vulgar-big. I wouldn't look like Giraffe--not for ever so.'

'I'll make 'em with the tips of my fingers,' said the Ethiopian. 'There's plenty of black left on my skin still. Stand over!'

Then the Ethiopian put his five fingers close together (there was plenty of black left on his new skin still) and pressed them all over the Leopard, and wherever the five fingers touched they left five little black marks, all close together. You can see them on any Leopard's skin you like, Best Beloved. Sometimes the fingers slipped and the marks got a little blurred; but if you look closely at any Leopard now you will see that there are always five spots--off five fat black finger-tips.

'Now you are a beauty!' said the Ethiopian. 'You can lie out on the bare ground and look like a heap of pebbles. You can lie out on the naked rocks and look like a piece of pudding-stone. You can lie out on a leafy branch and look like sunshine sifting through the leaves; and you can lie right across the centre of a path and look like nothing in particular. Think of that and purr!'

'But if I'm all this,' said the Leopard, 'why didn't you go spotty too?'

'Oh, plain black's best for me,' said the Ethiopian. 'Now come along and we'll see if we can't get even with Mr. One-Two-Three-Where's-your-Breakfast!'

So they went away and lived happily ever afterward, Best Beloved. That is all.

Oh, now and then you will hear grown-ups say, 'Can the Ethiopian change his skin or the Leopard his spots?' I don't think even grown-ups would keep on saying such a silly thing if the Leopard and the Ethiopian hadn't done it once--do you? But they will never do it again, Best Beloved. They are quite contented as they are.

I am the Most Wise Baviaan, saying in most wise tones, 'Let us melt into the landscape--just us two by our lones.' People have come--in a carriage--calling. But Mummy is there.... Yes, I can go if you take me--Nurse says she don't care. Let's go up to the pig-sties and sit on the farmyard rails! Let's say things to the bunnies, and watch 'em skitter their tails! Let's--oh, anything, daddy, so long as it's you and me, And going truly exploring, and not being in till tea! Here's your boots (I've brought 'em), and here's your cap and stick, And here's your pipe and tobacco. Oh, come along out of it --quick.

Rudyard Kipling – How the Leopard Got His Spots (1902)

Exercises

1. The word "fair" in line 1 means:
   A. impartial
   B. on equal terms
   C. blond
   D. matched
   E. just

2. The setting of the tale is:
   A. Indonesia
   B. India
   C. Ethiopia
   D. Sub-Saharan savannah
   E. South Africa

3. Baviaan is a:
   A. game warden
   B. wise tribesman
   C. bird
   D. baboon
   E. hyena

4. The Ethiopian rephrases Leopard's question (l. 74) because:
   A. Baviaan blinked
   B. Baviaan misunderstands
   C. he wants to seem intelligent
   D. Leopard's affected by the heat
   E. he likes hearing himself talk

5. As contrasts to darkness all of the following are mentioned except:
   A. sun-flowers
   B. soap
   C. mustard-plaster
   D. the moon
   E. bananas

6. The story-teller's purpose is to:
   A. ridicule evolution
   B. mock folktales
   C. entertain a child
   D. evoke African superstition
   E. explain coloration

7. The title alludes to the biblical - "Can a leopard change his spots?" as a way to:
   A. play verbal games
   B. discredit Biblical truth
   C. explain how camouflage works
   D. compare Darwinism to Bible accounts
   E. change his readers' minds

8. The "Best Beloved" seems to be the narrator's present:
   A. wife
   B. dog
   C. child
   D. companion
   E. tribesman

9. The word "fauna" refers to:
   A. undergrowth
   B. climate
   C. trees
   D. animals
   E. jungle tracks

10. The leopard's spots arise from:
    A. the forest
    B. the veldt
    C. ashes
    D. the Ethiopian's skin
    E. shadows in the jungle

KENNETH GRAHAME - WIND IN THE WILLOWS (1908)

THE RIVER BANK

The Mole had been working very hard all the morning, spring-cleaning his little home. First with brooms, then with dusters; then on ladders and steps and chairs, with a brush and a pail of whitewash; till he had dust in his throat and eyes, and splashes of whitewash all over his black fur, and an aching back and weary arms. Spring was moving in the air above and in the earth below and around him, penetrating even his dark and lowly little house with its spirit of divine discontent and longing. It was small wonder, then, that he suddenly flung down his brush on the floor, said `Bother!' and `O blow!' and also `Hang spring-cleaning!' and bolted out of the house without even waiting to put on his coat. Something up above was calling him imperiously, and he made for the steep little tunnel which answered in his case to the gravelled carriage-drive owned by animals whose residences are nearer to the sun and air. So he scraped and scratched and scrabbled and scrooged and then he scrooged again and scrabbled and scratched and scraped, working busily with his little paws and muttering to himself, `Up we go! Up we go!' till at last, pop! his snout came out into the sunlight, and he found himself rolling in the warm grass of a great meadow.

`This is fine!' he said to himself. `This is better than whitewashing!' The sunshine struck hot on his fur, soft breezes caressed his heated brow, and after the seclusion of the cellarage he had lived in so long the carol of happy birds fell on his dulled hearing almost like a shout. Jumping off all his four legs at once, in the joy of living and the delight of spring without its cleaning, he pursued his way across the meadow till he reached the hedge on the further side.

`Hold up!' said an elderly rabbit at the gap. `Sixpence for the privilege of passing by the private road!' He was bowled over in an instant by the impatient and contemptuous Mole, who trotted along the side of the hedge chaffing the other rabbits as they peeped hurriedly from their holes to see what the row was about. `Onion-sauce! Onion-sauce!' he remarked jeeringly, and was gone before they could think of a thoroughly satisfactory reply. Then they all started grumbling at each other. `How *stupid* you are! Why didn't you tell him -- -- ' `Well, why didn't *you* say -- -- ' `You might have reminded him -- -- ' and so on, in the usual way; but, of course, it was then much too late, as is always the case.

It all seemed too good to be true. Hither and thither through the meadows he rambled busily, along the hedgerows, across the copses, finding everywhere birds building, flowers budding, leaves thrusting -- everything happy, and progressive, and occupied. And instead of having an uneasy conscience pricking him and whispering `whitewash!' he somehow could only feel how jolly it was to be the only idle dog among all these busy citizens. After all, the best part of a holiday is perhaps not so much to be resting yourself, as to see all the other fellows busy working.

He thought his happiness was complete when, as he meandered aimlessly along, suddenly he stood by the edge of a full-fed river. Never in his life had he seen a river before -- this sleek, sinuous, full-bodied animal, chasing and chuckling, gripping things with a gurgle and leaving them with a laugh, to fling itself on fresh playmates that shook themselves free, and were caught and held again. All was a-shake and a-shiver -- glints and gleams and sparkles, rustle and swirl, chatter and bubble. The Mole was bewitched, entranced, fascinated. By the side of the river he trotted as one trots, when very small, by the side of a man who holds one spell-bound by exciting stories; and when tired at last, he sat on the bank, while the river still chattered on to him, a babbling procession of the best stories in the world, sent from the heart of the earth to be told at last to the insatiable sea.

As he sat on the grass and looked across the river, a dark hole in the bank opposite, just above the water's edge, caught his eye, and dreamily he fell to considering what a nice snug dwelling-place it would make for an animal with few wants and fond of a bijo riverside residence, above flood level and remote from noise and dust. As he gazed, something bright and small seemed to twinkle down in the heart of it, vanished, then twinkled once more like a tiny star. But it could hardly be a star in such an unlikely situation; and it was too glittering and small for a glow-worm. Then, as he looked, it winked at him, and so declared itself to be an eye; and a small face began gradually to grow up round it, like a frame round a picture.

A brown little face, with whiskers.

A grave round face, with the same twinkle in its eye that had first attracted his notice.

Small neat ears and thick silky hair.

It was the Water Rat!

Then the two animals stood and regarded each other cautiously.

`Hullo, Mole!' said the Water Rat.

`Hullo, Rat!' said the Mole.

`Would you like to come over?' enquired the Rat presently.

`Oh, its all very well to *talk*,' said the Mole, rather pettishly, he being new to a river and riverside life and its ways.

The Rat said nothing, but stooped and unfastened a rope and hauled on it; then lightly stepped into a little boat which the Mole had not observed. It was painted blue outside and white within, and was just the size for two animals; and the Mole's whole heart went out to it at once, even though he did not yet fully understand its uses.

The Rat sculled smartly across and made fast. Then he held up his forepaw as the

Mole stepped gingerly down. 'Lean on that!' he said. 'Now then, step lively!' and the Mole to his surprise and rapture found himself actually seated in the stern of a real boat.

'This has been a wonderful day!' said he, as the Rat shoved off and took to the sculls again. 'Do you know, I've never been in a boat before in all my life.'

'What?' cried the Rat, open-mouthed: 'Never been in a -- you never -- well I -- what have you been doing, then?'

'Is it so nice as all that?' asked the Mole shyly, though he was quite prepared to believe it as he leant back in his seat and surveyed the cushions, the oars, the rowlocks, and all the fascinating fittings, and felt the boat sway lightly under him.

'Nice? It's the *only* thing,' said the Water Rat solemnly, as he leant forward for his stroke. 'Believe me, my young friend, there is *nothing* -- absolute nothing -- half so much worth doing as simply messing about in boats. Simply messing,' he went on dreamily: 'messing -- about -- in -- boats; messing -- -- '

'Look ahead, Rat!' cried the Mole suddenly.

It was too late. The boat struck the bank full tilt. The dreamer, the joyous oarsman, lay on his back at the bottom of the boat, his heels in the air.

' -- about in boats -- or *with* boats,' the Rat went on composedly, picking himself up with a pleasant laugh. 'In or out of 'em, it doesn't matter. Nothing seems really to matter, that's the charm of it. Whether you get away, or whether you don't; whether you arrive at your destination or whether you reach somewhere else, or whether you never get anywhere at all, you're always busy, and you never do anything in particular; and when you've done it there's always something else to do, and you can do it if you like, but you'd much better not. Look here! If you've really nothing else on hand this morning, supposing we drop down the river together, and have a long day of it?'

The Mole waggled his toes from sheer happiness, spread his chest with a sigh of full contentment, and leaned back blissfully into the soft cushions. '*What* a day I'm having!' he said. 'Let us start at once!'

'Hold hard a minute, then!' said the Rat. He looped the painter through a ring in his landing-stage, climbed up into his hole above, and after a short interval reappeared staggering under a fat, wicker luncheon-basket.

'Shove that under your feet,' he observed to the Mole, as he passed it down into the boat. Then he untied the painter and took the sculls again.

'What's inside it?' asked the Mole, wriggling with curiosity.

'There's cold chicken inside it,' replied the Rat briefly; 'coldtonguecoldhamcoldbeefpickledgherkinssaladfrenchrollscresssandwichespottedmeatgingerbeerlemonadesodawater -- -- '

'O stop, stop,' cried the Mole in ecstacies: 'This is too much!'

'Do you really think so?' enquired the Rat seriously. 'It's only what I always take on these little excursions; and the other animals are always telling me that I'm a mean beast and cut it *very* fine!'

The Mole never heard a word he was saying. Absorbed in the new life he was entering upon, intoxicated with the sparkle, the ripple, the scents and the sounds and the sunlight, he trailed a paw in the water and dreamed long waking dreams. The Water Rat, like the good little fellow he was, sculled steadily on and forebore to disturb him.

'I like your clothes awfully, old chap,' he remarked after some half an hour or so had passed. 'I'm going to get a black velvet smoking-suit myself some day, as soon as I can afford it.'

'I beg your pardon,' said the Mole, pulling himself together with an effort. 'You must think me very rude; but all this is so new to me. So -- this -- is -- a -- River!'

'*The* River,' corrected the Rat.

'And you really live by the river? What a jolly life!'

'By it and with it and on it and in it,' said the Rat. 'It's brother and sister to me, and aunts, and company, and food and drink, and (naturally) washing. It's my world, and I don't want any other. What it hasn't got is not worth having, and what it doesn't know is not worth knowing. Lord! the times we've had together! Whether in winter or summer, spring or autumn, it's always got its fun and its excitements. When the floods are on in February, and my cellars and basement are brimming with drink that's no good to me, and the brown water runs by my best bedroom window; or again when it all drops away and, shows patches of mud that smells like plum-cake, and the rushes and weed clog the channels, and I can potter about dry shod over most of the bed of it and find fresh food to eat, and things careless people have dropped out of boats!'

'But isn't it a bit dull at times?' the Mole ventured to ask. 'Just you and the river, and no one else to pass a word with?'

'No one else to -- well, I mustn't be hard on you,' said the Rat with forbearance. 'You're new to it, and of course you don't know. The bank is so crowded nowadays that many people are moving away altogether: O no, it isn't what it used to be, at all. Otters, kingfishers, dabchicks, moorhens, all of them about all day long and always wanting you to *do* something -- as if a fellow had no business of his own to attend to!'

'What lies over *there?*' asked the Mole, waving a paw towards a background of woodland that darkly framed the water-meadows on one side of the river.

'That? O, that's just the Wild Wood,' said the Rat shortly. 'We don't go there very much, we river-bankers.'

'Aren't they -- aren't they very *nice* people in there?' said the Mole, a trifle nervously.

'W-e-ll,' replied the Rat, 'let me see. The squirrels are all right. *And* the rabbits -- some of 'em, but rabbits are a mixed lot. And then there's Badger, of course. He lives right in the heart of it; wouldn't live anywhere else, either, if you paid him to do it. Dear old Badger! Nobody interferes with *him*. They'd better not,' he added significantly.

'Why, who *should* interfere with him?' asked the Mole.

'Well, of course -- there -- are others,' explained the Rat in a hesitating sort of way.

'Weasels -- and stoats -- and foxes -- and so on. They're all right in a way -- I'm very good friends with them -- pass the time of day when we meet, and all that -- but they break out sometimes, there's no denying it, and then -- well, you can't really trust them, and that's the fact.'

The Mole knew well that it is quite against animal-etiquette to dwell on possible trouble ahead, or even to allude to it; so he dropped the subject.

'And beyond the Wild Wood again?' he asked: 'Where it's all blue and dim, and one sees what may be hills or perhaps they mayn't, and something like the smoke of towns, or is it only cloud-drift?'

'Beyond the Wild Wood comes the Wide World,' said the Rat. 'And that's something that doesn't matter, either to you or me. I've never been there, and I'm never going, nor you either, if you've got any sense at all.

Don't ever refer to it again, please. Now then! Here's our backwater at last, where we're going to lunch.'

Leaving the main stream, they now passed into what seemed at first sight like a little land-locked lake. Green turf sloped down to either edge, brown snaky tree-roots gleamed below the surface of the quiet water, while ahead of them the silvery shoulder and foamy tumble of a weir, arm-in-arm with a restless dripping mill-wheel, that held up in its turn a grey-gabled mill-house, filled the air with a soothing murmur of sound, dull and smothery, yet with little clear voices speaking up cheerfully out of it at intervals. It was so very beautiful that the Mole could only hold up both forepaws and gasp, `O my! O my! O my!'

The Rat brought the boat alongside the bank, made her fast, helped the still awkward Mole safely ashore, and swung out the luncheon-basket. The Mole begged as a favour to be allowed to unpack it all by himself; and the Rat was very pleased to indulge him, and to sprawl at full length on the grass and rest, while his excited friend shook out the table-cloth and spread it, took out all the mysterious packets one by one and arranged their contents in due order, still gasping, `O my! O my!' at each fresh revelation. When all was ready, the Rat said, `Now, pitch in, old fellow!' and the Mole was indeed very glad to obey, for he had started his spring-cleaning at a very early hour that morning, as people *will* do, and had not paused for bite or sup; and he had been through a very great deal since that distant time which now seemed so many days ago.

`What are you looking at?' said the Rat presently, when the edge of their hunger was somewhat dulled, and the Mole's eyes were able to wander off the table-cloth a little.

`I am looking,' said the Mole, `at a streak of bubbles that I see travelling along the surface of the water. That is a thing that strikes me as funny.'

`Bubbles? Oho!' said the Rat, and chirruped cheerily in an inviting sort of way.

A broad glistening muzzle showed itself above the edge of the bank, and the Otter hauled himself out and shook the water from his coat.

`Greedy beggars!' he observed, making for the provender. `Why didn't you invite me, Ratty?'

`This was an impromptu affair,' explained the Rat. `By the way -- my friend Mr. Mole.'

`Proud, I'm sure,' said the Otter, and the two animals were friends forthwith.

`Such a rumpus everywhere!' continued the Otter. `All the world seems out on the river to-day. I came up this backwater to try and get a moment's peace, and then stumble upon you fellows! -- At least -- I beg pardon -- I don't exactly mean that, you know.'

There was a rustle behind them, proceeding from a hedge wherein last year's leaves still clung thick, and a stripy head, with high shoulders behind it, peered forth on them.

`Come on, old Badger!' shouted the Rat.

The Badger trotted forward a pace or two; then grunted, `H'm! Company,' and turned his back and disappeared from view.

`That's *just* the sort of fellow he is!' observed the disappointed Rat. `Simply hates Society! Now we shan't see any more of him to-day. Well, tell us, *who's* out on the river?'

`Toad's out, for one,' replied the Otter. `In his brand-new wager-boat; new togs, new everything!'

The two animals looked at each other and laughed.

'Once, it was nothing but sailing,' said the Rat, 'Then he tired of that and took to punting.'

Nothing would please him but to punt all day and every day, and a nice mess he made of it. Last year it was house-boating, and we all had to go and stay with him in his house-boat, and pretend we liked it. He was going to spend the rest of his life in a house-boat. It's all the same, whatever he takes up; he gets tired of it, and starts on something fresh.'

'Such a good fellow, too,' remarked the Otter reflectively: 'But no stability -- especially in a boat!'

From where they sat they could get a glimpse of the main stream across the island that separated them; and just then a wager-boat flashed into view, the rower -- a short, stout figure -- splashing badly and rolling a good deal, but working his hardest. The Rat stood up and hailed him, but Toad -- for it was he -- shook his head and settled sternly to his work.

'He'll be out of the boat in a minute if he rolls like that,' said the Rat, sitting down again.

'Of course he will,' chuckled the Otter. 'Did I ever tell you that good story about Toad and the lock-keeper? It happened this way. Toad. . . .'

An errant May-fly swerved unsteadily athwart the current in the intoxicated fashion affected by young bloods of May-flies seeing life. A swirl of water and a `cloop!' and the May-fly was visible no more.

Neither was the Otter.

The Mole looked down. The voice was still in his ears, but the turf whereon he had sprawled was clearly vacant. Not an Otter to be seen, as far as the distant horizon.

But again there was a streak of bubbles on the surface of the river.

The Rat hummed a tune, and the Mole recollected that animal-etiquette forbade any sort of comment on the sudden disappearance of one's friends at any moment, for any reason or no reason whatever.

'Well, well,' said the Rat, 'I suppose we ought to be moving. I wonder which of us had better pack the luncheon-basket?' He did not speak as if he was frightfully eager for the treat.

'O, please let me,' said the Mole. So, of course, the Rat let him.

Packing the basket was not quite such pleasant work as unpacking' the basket. It never is. But the Mole was bent on enjoying everything, and although just when he had got the basket packed and strapped up tightly he saw a plate staring up at him from the grass, and when the job had been done again the Rat pointed out a fork which anybody ought to have seen, and last of all, behold! the mustard pot, which he had been sitting on without knowing it -- still, somehow, the thing got finished at last, without much loss of temper.

The afternoon sun was getting low as the Rat sculled gently homewards in a dreamy mood, murmuring poetry-things over to himself, and not paying much attention to Mole. But the Mole was very full of lunch, and self-satisfaction, and pride, and already quite at home in a boat (so he thought) and was getting a bit restless besides: and presently he said, 'Ratty! Please, *I* want to row, now!'

The Rat shook his head with a smile. 'Not yet, my young friend,' he said -- 'wait till you've had a few lessons. It's not so easy as it looks.'

The Mole was quiet for a minute or two. But he began to feel more and more jealous of Rat, sculling so strongly and so easily along, and his pride began to whisper that he could do it every bit as well. He jumped up and seized the sculls, so suddenly, that the Rat, who was gazing out over the water and saying more poetry-things to himself, was taken by surprise and fell backwards off his seat with his legs in the air for the second time, while the triumphant Mole took his place and grabbed the sculls with entire confidence.

'Stop it, you *silly* ass!' cried the Rat, from the bottom of the boat. 'You can't do it! You'll have us over!'

The Mole flung his sculls back with a flourish, and made a great dig at the water. He missed the surface altogether, his legs flew up above his head, and he found himself lying on the top of the prostrate Rat. Greatly alarmed, he made a grab at the side of the boat, and the next moment -- Sploosh!

Over went the boat, and he found himself struggling in the river.

O my, how cold the water was, and O, how *very* wet it felt. How it sang in his ears as he went down, down, down! How bright and welcome the sun looked as he rose to the surface coughing and spluttering! How black was his despair when he felt himself sinking again! Then a firm paw gripped him by the back of his neck. It was the Rat, and he was evidently laughing -- the Mole could *feel* him laughing, right down his arm and through his paw, and so into his -- the Mole's -- neck.

The Rat got hold of a scull and shoved it under the Mole's arm; then he did the same by the other side of him and, swimming behind, propelled the helpless animal to shore, hauled him out, and set him down on the bank, a squashy, pulpy lump of misery.

When the Rat had rubbed him down a bit, and wrung some of the wet out of him, he said, 'Now, then, old fellow! Trot up and down the towing-path as hard as you can, till you're warm and dry again, while I dive for the luncheon-basket.'

So the dismal Mole, wet without and ashamed within, trotted about till he was fairly dry, while the Rat plunged into the water again, recovered the boat, righted her and made her fast, fetched his floating property to shore by degrees, and finally dived successfully for the luncheon-basket and struggled to land with it.

When all was ready for a start once more, the Mole, limp and dejected, took his seat in the stern of the boat; and as they set off, he said in a low voice, broken with emotion, 'Ratty, my generous friend! I am very sorry indeed for my foolish and ungrateful conduct. My heart quite fails me when I think how I might have lost that beautiful luncheon-basket. Indeed, I have been a complete ass, and I know it. Will you overlook it this once and forgive me, and let things go on as before?'

'That's all right, bless you!' responded the Rat cheerily. 'What's a little wet to a Water Rat? I'm more in the water than out of it most days. Don't you think any more about it; and, look here! I really think you had better come and stop with me for a little time. It's very plain and rough, you know -- not like Toad's house at all -- but you haven't seen that yet; still, I can make you comfortable. And I'll teach you to row, and to swim, and you'll soon be as handy on the water as any of us.'

The Mole was so touched by his kind manner of speaking that he could find no voice to answer him; and he had to brush away a tear or two with the back of his paw. But the Rat kindly looked in another direction, and presently the Mole's spirits revived again, and he was even able to give some straight back-talk to a couple of moorhens who were sniggering to each other about his bedraggled appearance.

When they got home, the Rat made a bright fire in the parlour, and planted the Mole in an arm-chair in front of it, having fetched down a dressing-gown and slippers for him, and told him river stories till supper-time. Very thrilling stories they were, too, to an earth-dwelling animal like Mole. Stories about weirs, and sudden floods, and leaping pike, and steamers that flung hard bottles -- at least bottles were certainly flung, and *from* steamers, so presumably *by* them; and about herons, and how particular they were whom they spoke to; and about adventures down drains, and night-fishings with Otter, or excursions far a-field with Badger. Supper was a most cheerful meal; but very shortly afterwards a terribly sleepy Mole had to be escorted upstairs by his considerate host, to the best bedroom, where he soon laid his head on his pillow in great peace and contentment, knowing that his new-found friend the River was lapping the sill of his window.

This day was only the first of many similar ones for the emancipated Mole, each of them longer and full of interest as the ripening summer moved onward. He learnt to swim and to row, and entered into the joy of running water; and with his ear to the reed-stems he caught, at intervals, something of what the wind went whispering so constantly among them.

Kenneth Grahame - *Wind in the Willows (1908)*

Exercises

1. The Mole is all of the following except:
   A. impatient
   B. contemptuous
   C. delighted at spring
   D. helpful
   E. adventurous

2. The Rat lives:
   A. in a riverbank
   B. on a boat
   C. upriver from Mole
   D. on the river
   E. under a log

3. In "The Rat ...made fast" (line 135-6) means the Rat:
   A. hadn't eaten
   B. hurried up
   C. tied up
   D. created quickly
   E. thought quickly

4. Rat claims that *nothing* compares to:
   A. a picnic lunch
   B. messing around in boats
   C. living on a river
   D. basking in the sun
   E. Toad's schemes

5. To Rat, the river represents all of the following except:
   A. food
   B. a close relative
   C. a bath
   D. excitement
   E. a mother

6. Rat says life on the river is worsening because of:
   A. flooding
   B. drought
   C. dams
   D. population
   E. his getting older

7. One can infer that Toad is:
   A. anti-social
   B. reckless
   C. not Otter's friend
   D. predictable
   E. a lady's man

8. Mole's is having his first encounter with:
   A. spring cleaning
   B. daylight
   C. a roadway
   D. grass
   E. a river

9. Rabbit is:
   A. a gatekeeper
   B. a game warden
   C. mute
   D. a tunneler
   E. asleep

10. Mole is called a "silly ass" for:
    A. talking nonsense
    B. sinking the boat
    C. trying to row
    D. not listening
    E. the lunch he has brought

SAKI – THE INTERLOPERS (1919)

In a forest of mixed growth somewhere on the eastern spurs of the Karpathians, a man stood one winter night watching and listening, as though he waited for some beast of the woods to come within the range of his vision, and, later, of his rifle. But the game for whose presence he kept so keen an outlook was none that figured in the sportsman's calendar as lawful and proper for the chase; Ulrich von Gradwitz patrolled the dark forest in quest of a human enemy.

The forest lands of Gradwitz were of wide extent and well stocked with game; the narrow strip of precipitous woodland that lay on its outskirt was not remarkable for the game it harboured or the shooting it afforded, but it was the most jealously guarded of all its owner's territorial possessions. A famous law suit, in the days of his grandfather, had wrested it from the illegal possession of a neighbouring family of petty landowners; the dispossessed party had never acquiesced in the judgment of the Courts, and a long series of poaching affrays and similar scandals had embittered the relationships between the families for three generations. The neighbour feud had grown into a personal one since Ulrich had come to be head of his family; if there was a man in the world whom he detested and wished ill to it was Georg Znaeym, the inheritor of the quarrel and the tireless game-snatcher and raider of the disputed borderforest. The feud might, perhaps, have died down or been compromised if the personal ill-will of the two men had not stood in the way; as boys they had thirsted for one another's blood, as men each prayed that misfortune might fall on the other, and this wind-scourged winter night Ulrich had banded together his foresters to watch the dark forest, not in quest of four-footed quarry, but to keep a look-out for the prowling thieves whom he suspected of being afoot from across the land boundary. The roebuck, which usually kept in the sheltered hollows during a storm-wind, were running like driven things to-night, and there was movement and unrest among the creatures that were wont to sleep through the dark hours. Assuredly there was a disturbing element in the forest, and Ulrich could guess the quarter from whence it came.

He strayed away by himself from the watchers whom he had placed in ambush on the crest of the hill, and wandered far down the steep slopes amid the wild tangle of undergrowth, peering through the tree trunks and listening through the whistling and skirling of the wind and the restless beating of the branches for sight and sound of the marauders. If only on this wild night, in this dark, lone spot, he might come across Georg Znaeym, man to man, with none to witness - that was the wish that was uppermost in his thoughts. And as he stepped round the trunk of a huge beech he came face to face with the man he sought.

The two enemies stood glaring at one another for a long silent moment. Each had a rifle in his hand, each had hate in his heart and murder uppermost in his mind. The chance had come to give full play to the passions of a lifetime. But a man who has been brought up under the code of a restraining civilisation cannot easily nerve himself to shoot down his neighbour in cold blood and without word spoken, except for an offence against his hearth and honour. And before the moment of hesitation had given way to action a deed of Nature's own violence overwhelmed them both. A fierce shriek of the storm had been answered by a splitting crash over their heads, and ere they could leap aside a mass of falling beech tree had thundered down on them. Ulrich von Gradwitz found himself stretched on the ground, one arm numb beneath him and the other held almost as helplessly in a tight tangle of forked branches, while both legs were pinned beneath the fallen mass. His heavy shooting-boots had saved his feet from being crushed to pieces, but if his fractures were not as serious as they might have been, at least it was evident that he could not move from his present position till some one came to release him. The descending twig had slashed the skin of his face, and he had to wink away some drops of blood from his eyelashes before he could take in a general view of the disaster. At his side, so near that under ordinary circumstances he could almost have touched him, lay Georg Znaeym, alive and struggling, but obviously as helplessly pinioned down as himself. All round them lay a thick-strewn wreckage of splintered branches and broken twigs.

Relief at being alive and exasperation at his captive plight brought a strange medley of pious thank-offerings and sharp curses to Ulrich's lips. Georg, who was early blinded with the blood which trickled across his eyes, stopped his struggling for a moment to listen, and then gave a short, snarling laugh.

"So you're not killed, as you ought to be, but you're caught, anyway," he cried; "caught fast. Ho, what a jest, Ulrich von Gradwitz snared in his stolen forest. There's real justice for you!"

And he laughed again, mockingly and savagely.

"I'm caught in my own forest-land," retorted Ulrich. "When my men come to release us you will wish, perhaps, that you were in a better plight than caught poaching on a neighbour's land, shame on you."

Georg was silent for a moment; then he answered quietly:

"Are you sure that your men will find much to release? I have men, too, in the forest tonight, close behind me, and THEY will be here first and do the releasing. When they drag me out from under these damned branches it won't need much clumsiness on their part to roll this mass of trunk right over on the top of you. Your men will find you dead under a fallen beech tree. For form's sake I shall send my condolences to your family."

"It is a useful hint," said Ulrich fiercely. "My men had orders to follow in ten minutes time, seven of which must have gone by already, and when they get me out - I will remember the hint. Only as you will have met your death poaching on my lands I don't think I can decently send any message of condolence to your family."

"Good," snarled Georg, "good. We fight this quarrel out to the death, you and I and our foresters, with no cursed interlopers to come between us. Death and damnation to you, Ulrich von Gradwitz."

"The same to you, Georg Znaeym, forest-thief, game-snatcher."

Both men spoke with the bitterness of possible defeat before them, for each knew that it might be long before his men would seek him out or find him; it was a bare matter of chance which party would arrive first on the scene.

Both had now given up the useless struggle to free themselves from the mass of wood that held them down; Ulrich limited his endeavours to an effort to bring his one partially free arm near enough to his outer coat-pocket to draw out his wine-flask. Even when he had accomplished that operation it was long before he could manage the unscrewing of the stopper or get any of the liquid down his throat. But what a Heaven-sent draught it seemed! It was an open winter, and little snow had fallen as yet, hence the captives suffered less from the cold than might have been the case at that season of the year; nevertheless, the wine was warming and reviving to the wounded man, and he looked across with something like a throb of pity to where his enemy lay, just keeping the groans of pain and weariness from crossing his lips.

"Could you reach this flask if I threw it over to you?" asked Ulrich suddenly; "there is good wine in it, and one may as well be as comfortable as one can. Let us drink, even if to-night one of us dies."

"No, I can scarcely see anything; there is so much blood caked round my eyes," said Georg, "and in any case I don't drink wine with an enemy."

Ulrich was silent for a few minutes, and lay listening to the weary screeching of the wind. An idea was slowly forming and growing in his brain, an idea that gained strength every time that he looked across at the man who was fighting so grimly against pain and exhaustion. In the pain and languor that Ulrich himself was feeling the old fierce hatred seemed to be dying down.

"Neighbour," he said presently, "do as you please if your men come first. It was a fair compact. But as for me, I've changed my mind. If my men are the first to come you shall be the first to be helped, as though you were my guest. We have quarrelled like devils all our lives over this stupid strip of forest, where the trees can't even stand upright in a breath of wind. Lying here to-night thinking I've come to think we've been rather fools; there are better things in life than getting the better of a boundary dispute. Neighbour, if you will help me to bury the old quarrel I - I will ask you to be my friend."

Georg Znaeym was silent for so long that Ulrich thought, perhaps, he had fainted with the pain of his injuries. Then he spoke slowly and in jerks.

"How the whole region would stare and gabble if we rode into the market-square together. No one living can remember seeing a Znaeym and a von Gradwitz talking to one another in friendship. And what peace there would be among the forester folk if we ended our feud to-night. And if we choose to make peace among our people there is none other to interfere, no interlopers from outside ... You would come and keep the Sylvester night beneath my roof, and I would come and feast on some high day at your castle ... I would never fire a shot on your land, save when you invited me as a guest; and you should come and shoot with me down in the marshes where the wildfowl are. In all the countryside there are none that could hinder if we willed to make peace. I never thought to have wanted to do other than hate you all my life, but I think I have changed my mind about things too, this last half-hour. And you offered me your wineflask ... Ulrich von Gradwitz, I will be your friend."

For a space both men were silent, turning over in their minds the wonderful changes that this dramatic reconciliation would bring about. In the cold, gloomy forest, with the wind tearing in fitful gusts through the naked branches and whistling round the tree-trunks, they lay and waited for the help that would now bring release and succour to both parties. And each prayed a private prayer that his men might be the first to arrive, so that he might be the first to show honourable attention to the enemy that had become a friend.

Presently, as the wind dropped for a moment, Ulrich broke silence.

"Let's shout for help," he said; he said; "in this lull our voices may carry a little way."

"They won't carry far through the trees and undergrowth," said Georg, "but we can try. Together, then."

The two raised their voices in a prolonged hunting call.

"Together again," said Ulrich a few minutes later, after listening in vain for an answering halloo.

"I heard nothing but the pestilential wind," said Georg hoarsely.

There was silence again for some minutes, and then Ulrich gave a joyful cry.

"I can see figures coming through the wood. They are following in the way I came down the hillside."

Both men raised their voices in as loud a shout as they could muster.

"They hear us! They've stopped. Now they see us. They're running down the hill towards us," cried Ulrich.

"How many of them are there?" asked Georg.

"I can't see distinctly," said Ulrich; "nine or ten,"

"Then they are yours," said Georg; "I had only seven out with me."

"They are making all the speed they can, brave lads," said Ulrich gladly.

"Are they your men?" asked Georg. "Are they your men?" he repeated impatiently as Ulrich did not answer.

"No," said Ulrich with a laugh, the idiotic chattering laugh of a man unstrung with hideous fear.

"Who are they?" asked Georg quickly, straining his eyes to see what the other would gladly not have seen.

"Wolves."

Saki – The Interlopers (1919)

Exercises

1. The setting of the story is a forest in:
   A. Eastern Europe
   B. Switzerland
   C. Scandinavia
   D. Germany
   E. Great Britain

2. The land is being fought over primarily because it:
   A. is good land for shooting game
   B. provides a steep border against poachers
   C. offers exceptional timber
   D. acts as a buffer zone
   E. serves as a symbol of mutual hatred

3. The word "interloper" most nearly means:
   A. outsider
   B. poacher
   C. mediator
   D. intruder
   E. interrupter

4. Ulrich is by himself in the woods because he:
   A. wants no witnesses
   B. has outdistanced his men
   C. has his men waiting in ambush
   D. wants to confront his enemy alone
   E. intends to cross into his enemy's land

5. Ulrich and Georg don't shoot each other immediately on sight because they:
   A. are mutually stunned
   B. are standing too close together
   C. have no men near to back them up
   D. get stopped by Mother Nature
   E. are gentleman

6. After carrying out his plan to kill Georg, Ulrich says he won't send condolences to Georg's family because Ulrich:
   A. considers Georg a poacher
   B. despises his enemy's family name
   C. has a sense of honor
   D. won't act like a hypocrite
   E. considers Ulrich ungentlemanly

7. The main irony in the story is that:
   A. the wolves will put an end the feud
   B. the feud was ultimately unnecessary
   C. the men's shouts for help attract wolves
   D. reconciliation comes too late
   E. violence triumphs over good will

8. The feud arose from a:
   A. series of paching afrays
   B. hunting accident
   C. contested will
   D. an interfamilial marriage
   E. lawsuit

9. Ulrich is in the woods in order to:
   A. hunt deer
   B. exercise his hunting dog
   C. fell trees
   D. set a boundary marker
   E. check for thieves

10. In line 232, the word "Sylvester" refers to a:
    A. feast day
    B. castle
    C. type of wine
    D. forest
    E. winter weather

AMERICAN LITERATURE

Edgar Allan Poe - The Tell-Tale Heart (1843)

EDGAR ALLAN POE - THE TELL-TALE HEART (1843)

TRUE! - nervous - very, very dreadfully nervous I had been and am; but why will you say that I am mad? The disease had sharpened my senses - not destroyed - not dulled them. Above all was the sense of hearing acute. I heard all things in the heaven and in the earth. I heard many things in hell. How, then, am I mad? Hearken! and observe how healthily - how calmly I can tell you the whole story.

It is impossible to say how first the idea entered my brain; but once conceived, it haunted me day and night. Object there was none. Passion there was none. I loved the old man. He had never wronged me. He had never given me insult. For his gold I had no desire. I think it was his eye! yes, it was this! He had the eye of a vulture - a pale blue eye, with a film over it. Whenever it fell upon me, my blood ran cold; and so by degrees - very gradually - I made up my mind to take the life of the old man, and thus rid myself of the eye forever.

Now this is the point. You fancy me mad. Madmen know nothing. But you should have seen me. You should have seen how wisely I proceeded - with what caution - with what foresight - with what dissimulation I went to work! I was never kinder to the old man than during the whole week before I killed him. And every night, about midnight, I turned the latch of his door and opened it - oh so gently! And then, when I had made an opening sufficient for my head, I put in a dark lantern, all closed, closed, that no light shone out, and then I thrust in my head. Oh, you would have laughed to see how cunningly I thrust it in! I moved it slowly - very, very slowly, so that I might not disturb the old man's sleep. It took me an hour to place my whole head within the opening so far that I could see him as he lay upon his bed. Ha! would a madman have been so wise as this, And then, when my head was well in the room, I undid the lantern cautiously-oh, so cautiously - cautiously (for the hinges creaked) - I undid it just so much that a single thin ray fell upon the vulture eye. And this I did for seven long nights - every night just at midnight - but I found the eye always closed; and so it was impossible to do the work; for it was not the old man who vexed me, but his Evil Eye. And every morning, when the day broke, I went boldly into the chamber, and spoke courageously to him, calling him by name in a hearty tone, and inquiring how he has passed the night. So you see he would have been a very profound old man, indeed, to suspect that every night, just at twelve, I looked in upon him while he slept.

Upon the eighth night I was more than usually cautious in opening the door. A watch's minute hand moves more quickly than did mine. Never before that night had I felt the extent of my own powers - of my sagacity. I could scarcely contain my feelings of triumph. To think that there I was, opening the door, little by little, and he not even to dream of my secret deeds or thoughts. I fairly chuckled at the idea; and perhaps he heard me; for he moved on the bed suddenly, as if startled. Now you may think that I drew back - but no. His room was as black as pitch with the thick darkness, (for the shutters were close fastened, through fear of robbers,) and so I knew that he could not see the opening of the door, and I kept pushing it on steadily, steadily.

I had my head in, and was about to open the lantern, when my thumb slipped upon the tin fastening, and the old man sprang up in bed, crying out - "Who's there?"

I kept quite still and said nothing. For a whole hour I did not move a muscle, and in the meantime I did not hear him lie down. He was still sitting up in the bed listening; - just as I have done, night after night, hearkening to the death watches in the wall.

Presently I heard a slight groan, and I knew it was the groan of mortal terror. It was not a groan of pain or of grief - oh, no! - it was the low stifled sound that arises from the bottom of the soul when overcharged with awe. I knew the sound well. Many a night, just at midnight, when all the world slept, it has welled up from my own bosom, deepening, with its dreadful echo, the terrors that distracted me. I say I knew it well. I knew what the old man felt, and pitied him, although I chuckled at heart. I knew that he had been lying awake ever since the first slight noise, when he had turned in the bed. His fears had been ever since growing upon him. He had been trying to fancy them causeless, but could not. He had been saying to himself - "It is nothing but the wind in the chimney - it is only a mouse crossing the floor," or "It is merely a cricket which has made a single chirp." Yes, he had been trying to comfort himself with these suppositions: but he had found all in vain. All in vain; because Death, in approaching him had stalked with his black shadow before him, and enveloped the victim. And it was the mournful influence of the unperceived shadow that caused him to feel - although he neither saw nor heard - to feel the presence of my head within the room.

When I had waited a long time, very patiently, without hearing him lie down, I resolved to open a little - a very, very little crevice in the lantern. So I opened it - you cannot imagine how stealthily, stealthily - until, at length a simple dim ray, like the thread of the spider, shot from out the crevice and fell full upon the vulture eye.

It was open - wide, wide open - and I grew furious as I gazed upon it. I saw it with perfect distinctness - all a dull blue, with a hideous veil over it that chilled the very marrow in my bones; but I could see nothing else of the old man's face or person: for I had directed the ray as if by instinct, precisely upon the damned spot.

And have I not told you that what you mistake for madness is but over-acuteness of the sense? - now, I say, there came to my ears a low, dull, quick sound, such as a watch makes when enveloped in cotton. I knew that sound well, too. It was the beating of the old man's heart. It increased my fury, as the beating of a drum stimulates the soldier into courage.

But even yet I refrained and kept still. I scarcely breathed. I held the lantern motionless. I tried how steadily I could maintain the ray upon the eve. Meantime the hellish tattoo of the heart increased. It grew quicker and quicker, and louder and louder every instant. The old man's terror must have been extreme! It grew louder, I say, louder every moment! - do you mark me well I have told you that I am nervous: so I am. And now at the dead hour of the night, amid the dreadful silence of that old house, so strange a noise as this excited me to uncontrollable terror. Yet, for some minutes longer I refrained and stood still. But the beating grew louder, louder! I thought the heart must burst. And now a new anxiety seized me - the sound would be heard by a neighbour! The old man's hour had come! With a loud yell, I threw open the lantern and leaped into the room. He shrieked once - once only. In an instant I dragged him to the floor, and pulled the heavy bed over him. I then smiled gaily, to find the deed so far done. But, for many minutes, the heart beat on with a muffled sound. This, however, did not vex me; it would not be heard through the wall. At length it ceased. The old man was dead. I removed the bed and examined the corpse. Yes, he was stone, stone dead. I placed my hand upon the heart and held it there many minutes. There was no pulsation. He was stone dead. His eye would trouble me no more.

If still you think me mad, you will think so no longer when I describe the wise precautions I took for the concealment of the body. The night waned, and I worked hastily, but in silence. First of all I dismembered the corpse. I cut off the head and the arms and the legs.

I then took up three planks from the flooring of the chamber, and deposited all between the scantlings. I then replaced the boards so cleverly, so cunningly, that no human eye - not even his - could have detected any thing wrong. There was nothing to wash out - no stain of any kind - no blood-spot whatever. I had been too wary for that. A tub had caught all - ha! ha!

When I had made an end of these labors, it was four o'clock - still dark as midnight. As the bell sounded the hour, there came a knocking at the street door. I went down to open it with a light heart, - for what had I now to fear? There entered three men, who introduced themselves, with perfect suavity, as officers of the police. A shriek had been heard by a neighbor during the night; suspicion of foul play had been aroused; information had been lodged at the police office, and they (the officers) had been deputed to search the premises.

I smiled, - for what had I to fear? I bade the gentlemen welcome. The shriek, I said, was my own in a dream. The old man, I mentioned, was absent in the country. I took my visitors all over the house. I bade them search - search well. I led them, at length, to his chamber. I showed them his treasures, secure, undisturbed. In the enthusiasm of my confidence, I brought chairs into the room, and desired them here to rest from their fatigues, while I myself, in the wild audacity of my perfect triumph, placed my own seat upon the very spot beneath which reposed the corpse of the victim.

The officers were satisfied. My manner had convinced them. I was singularly at ease. They sat, and while I answered cheerily, they chatted of familiar things. But, ere long, I felt myself getting pale and wished them gone. My head ached, and I fancied a ringing in my ears: but still they sat and still chatted. The ringing became more distinct: - It continued and became more distinct: I talked more freely to get rid of the feeling: but it continued and gained definiteness - until, at length, I found that the noise was not within my ears.

No doubt I now grew very pale; - but I talked more fluently, and with a heightened voice. Yet the sound increased - and what could I do? It was a low, dull, quick sound - much such a sound as a watch makes when enveloped in cotton. I gasped for breath - and yet the officers heard it not. I talked more quickly - more vehemently; but the noise steadily increased. I arose and argued about trifles, in a high key and with violent gesticulations; but the noise steadily increased. Why would they not be gone? I paced the floor to and fro with heavy strides, as if excited to fury by the observations of the men - but the noise steadily increased. Oh God! what could I do? I foamed - I raved - I swore! I swung the chair upon which I had been sitting, and grated it upon the boards, but the noise arose over all and continually increased. It grew louder - louder - louder! And still the men chatted pleasantly, and smiled. Was it possible they heard not? Almighty God! - no, no! They heard! - they suspected! - they knew! - they were making a mockery of my horror!-this I thought, and this I think. But anything was better than this agony! Anything was more tolerable than this derision! I could bear those hypocritical smiles no longer! I felt that I must scream or die! and now - again! - hark! louder! louder! louder! louder!

"Villains!" I shrieked, "dissemble no more! I admit the deed! - tear up the planks! here, here! - It is the beating of his hideous heart!"

Edgar Allan Poe - The Tell-Tale Heart (1843)

Exercises

1. The narrator considers himself as all of the following except:
   A. acute of hearing
   B. cunning
   C. nervous
   D. obsessive
   E. mad

2. What fixates the narrator on his neighbor:
   A. an imagined insult
   B. the old man's hypocritical friendliness
   C. an evil eye
   D. a ticking watch
   E. a beating heart

3. For seven days running the narrator fails to:
   A. summon the nerve to kill
   B. enter his neighbor's room
   C. find the old man awake at midnight
   D. talk to his neighbor
   E. enter the old man's room at night

4. The eighth night differed from prior nights in all the following ways except that the:
   A. old man moved in bed
   B. old man awoke
   C. narrator opened the lantern
   D. narrator crept more cautiously
   E. narrator heard the old man's heart

5. In line 150, the word "tattoo" means:
   A. an indelible mark
   B. a thump
   C. crescendo
   D. rhythmic tapping
   E. scar

6. The police arrive as the result of their:
   A. hearing the narrator's yell
   B. hearing the heavy furniture being moved
   C. hearing the old man's shriek
   D. hearing a neighbor's story
   E. superior's order

7. The officers were smiling at the end because they:
   A. found everything normal
   B. had entrapped the narrator
   C. found the narrator's behavior curious
   D. were pretending nothing was wrong
   E. thought the narrator delusional

8. The old man's groan arises from
   A. pain
   B. a nightmare
   C. grief
   D. fear
   E. the narrator's attack

9. The narrator eventually does this to the old man:
   A. crushes him
   B. strangles him
   C. suffocates him
   D. stuffs him in a closet
   E. stabs him

10. The passage is best described as this kind of story:
    A. science fiction
    B. detective
    C. police procedural
    D. horror
    E. suspense

Herman Melville - Moby Dick (1851)

Chapter 1 - LOOMINGS

Call me Ishmael. Some years ago - never mind how long precisely - having little or no money in my purse, and nothing particu-
5 lar to interest me on shore, I thought I would sail about a little and see the watery part of the world. It is a way I have of driving off the spleen, and regulating the circulation. Whenever I find myself growing
10 grim about the mouth; whenever it is a damp, drizzly November in my soul; whenever I find myself involuntarily pausing before coffin warehouses, and bringing up the rear of every funeral I meet; and especially
15 whenever my hypos get such an upper hand of me, that it requires a strong moral principle to prevent me from deliberately stepping into the street, and methodically knocking people's hats off - then, I account
20 it high time to get to sea as soon as I can. This is my substitute for pistol and ball. With a philosophical flourish Cato throws himself upon his sword; I quietly take to the ship. There is nothing surprising in this.

25 If they but knew it, almost all men in their degree, some time or other, cherish very nearly the same feelings towards the ocean with me.

There now is your insular city of the Man-
30 hattoes, belted round by wharves as Indian isles by coral reefs - commerce surrounds it with her surf. Right and left, the streets take you waterward. Its extreme down-town is the battery, where that noble mole is
35 washed by waves, and cooled by breezes, which a few hours previous were out of sight of land. Look at the crowds of water-gazers there.

Circumambulate the city of a dreamy Sab-
40 bath afternoon. Go from Corlears Hook to Coenties Slip, and from thence, by Whitehall northward. What do you see? - Posted like silent sentinels all around the town, stand thousands upon thousands of mortal
45 men fixed in ocean reveries. Some leaning against the spiles; some seated upon the pier-heads; some looking over the bulwarks of ships from China; some high aloft in the

Herman Melville - Moby Dick (1851)

rigging, as if striving to get a still better
seaward peep. But these are all landsmen;
of week days pent up in lath and plaster -
tied to counters, nailed to benches, clinched
to desks. How then is this? Are the green
fields gone? What do they here?

But look! here come more crowds, pacing
straight for the water, and seemingly bound
for a dive. Strange! Nothing will content
them but the extremest limit of the land;
loitering under the shady lee of yonder
warehouses will not suffice. No. They must
get just as nigh the water as they possibly
can without falling in. And there they stand
- miles of them - leagues. Inlanders all, they
come from lanes and alleys, streets and avenues,
- north, east, south, and west. Yet
here they all unite. Tell me, does the magnetic
virtue of the needles of the compasses
of all those ships attract them thither?

Once more. Say, you are in the country; in
some high land of lakes. Take almost any
path you please, and ten to one it carries
you down in a dale, and leaves you there by
a pool in the stream. There is magic in it.
Let the most absent- minded of men be
plunged in his deepest reveries - stand that
man on his legs, set his feet a-going, and he
will infallibly lead you to water, if water
there be in all that region. Should you ever
be athirst in the great American desert, try
this experiment, if your caravan happen to
be supplied with a metaphysical professor.
Yes, as every one knows, meditation and
water are wedded for ever.

But here is an artist. He desires to paint you
the dreamiest, shadiest, quietest, most enchanting
bit of romantic landscape in all
the valley of the Saco. What is the chief element
he employs? There stand his trees,
each with a hollow trunk, as if a hermit and
a crucifix were within; and here sleeps his
meadow, and there sleep his cattle; and up
from yonder cottage goes a sleepy smoke.
Deep into distant woodlands winds a mazy
way, reaching to overlapping spurs of
mountains bathed in their hill-side blue.
But though the picture lies thus tranced,
and though this pine-tree shakes down its
sighs like leaves upon this shepherd's head,
yet all were vain, unless the shepherd's eye
were fixed upon the magic stream before
him. Go visit the Prairies in June, when for
scores on scores of miles you wade knee-deep
among Tiger- lilies - what is the one
charm wanting? - Water - there is not a
drop of water there! Were Niagara but a
cataract of sand, would you travel your
thousand miles to see it? Why did the poor
poet of Tennessee, upon suddenly receiving
two handfuls of silver, deliberate whether
to buy him a coat, which he sadly needed,
or invest his money in a pedestrian trip to
Rockaway Beach? Why is almost every robust
healthy boy with a robust healthy soul
in him, at some time or other crazy to go to
sea? Why upon your first voyage as a passenger,
did you yourself feel such a mystical
vibration, when first told that you and
your ship were now out of sight of land?
Why did the old Persians hold the sea holy?
Why did the Greeks give it a separate deity,
and own brother of Jove? Surely all this is
not without meaning. And still deeper the
meaning of that story of Narcissus, who because
he could not grasp the tormenting,
mild image he saw in the fountain, plunged
into it and was drowned. But that same image,
we ourselves see in all rivers and
oceans. It is the image of the ungraspable
phantom of life; and this is the key to it all.

Now, when I say that I am in the habit of
going to sea whenever I begin to grow hazy
about the eyes, and begin to be over conscious
of my lungs, I do not mean to have it
inferred that I ever go to sea as a passenger.
For to go as a passenger you must needs
have a purse, and a purse is but a rag unless
you have something in it. Besides, passengers
get sea-sick - grow quarrelsome - don't
sleep of nights - do not enjoy themselves
much, as a general thing; - no, I never go as
a passenger; nor, though I am something of

a salt, do I ever go to sea as a Commodore, or a Captain, or a Cook. I abandon the glory and distinction of such offices to those who like them. For my part, I abominate all honorable respectable toils, trials, and tribulations of every kind whatsoever. It is quite as much as I can do to take care of myself, without taking care of ships, barques, brigs, schooners, and what not. And as for going as cook, - though I confess there is considerable glory in that, a cook being a sort of officer on ship-board - yet, somehow, I never fancied broiling fowls; - though once broiled, judiciously buttered, and judgmatically salted and peppered, there is no one who will speak more respectfully, not to say reverentially, of a broiled fowl than I will. It is out of the idolatrous dotings of the old Egyptians upon broiled ibis and roasted river horse, that you see the mummies of those creatures in their huge bake-houses the pyramids.

No, when I go to sea, I go as a simple sailor, right before the mast, plumb down into the forecastle, aloft there to the royal mast-head. True, they rather order me about some, and make me jump from spar to spar, like a grasshopper in a May meadow. And at first, this sort of thing is unpleasant enough. It touches one's sense of honor, particularly if you come of an old established family in the land, the van Rensselaers, or Randolphs, or Hardicanutes. And more than all, if just previous to putting your hand into the tar-pot, you have been lording it as a country schoolmaster, making the tallest boys stand in awe of you. The transition is a keen one, I assure you, from the schoolmaster to a sailor, and requires a strong decoction of Seneca and the Stoics to enable you to grin and bear it. But even this wears off in time.

What of it, if some old hunks of a sea-captain orders me to get a broom and sweep down the decks? What does that indignity amount to, weighed, I mean, in the scales of the New Testament? Do you think the archangel Gabriel thinks anything the less of me, because I promptly and respectfully obey that old hunks in that particular instance? Who aint a slave? Tell me that. Well, then, however the old sea-captains may order me about - however they may thump and punch me about, I have the satisfaction of knowing that it is all right; that everybody else is one way or other served in much the same way - either in a physical or metaphysical point of view, that is; and so the universal thump is passed round, and all hands should rub each other's shoulder-blades, and be content.

Again, I always go to sea as a sailor, because they make a point of paying me for my trouble, whereas they never pay passengers a single penny that I ever heard of. On the contrary, passengers themselves must pay. And there is all the difference in the world between paying and being paid. The act of paying is perhaps the most uncomfortable infliction that the two orchard thieves entailed upon us. But being paid, - what will compare with it? The urbane activity with which a man receives money is really marvellous, considering that we so earnestly believe money to be the root of all earthly ills, and that on no account can a monied man enter heaven. Ah! how cheerfully we consign ourselves to perdition!

Finally, I always go to sea as a sailor, because of the wholesome exercise and pure air of the forecastle deck. For as in this world, head winds are far more prevalent than winds from astern (that is, if you never violate the Pythagorean maxim), so for the most part the Commodore on the quarter-deck gets his atmosphere at second hand from the sailors on the forecastle. He thinks he breathes it first; but not so. In much the same way do the commonalty lead their leaders in many other things, at the same time that the leaders little suspect it. But wherefore it was that after having repeatedly smelt the sea as a merchant sailor, I should now take it into my head to go on a whaling voyage; this the invisible police officer of the Fates, who has the constant surveillance of me, and secretly dogs me, and influences me in some unaccountable way - he can better answer than any one else. And, doubtless, my going on this whaling voyage, formed part of the grand programme of Providence that was drawn up a long time ago. It came in as a sort of brief interlude and solo between more extensive performances. I take it that this part of the bill must have run something like this:

Grand Contested Election for the Presidency of the United States

Whaling Voyage by one Ishmael BLOODY BATTLE IN AFGHANISTAN Though I

cannot tell why it was exactly that those stage managers, the Fates, put me down for this shabby part of a whaling voyage, when others were set down for magnificent parts in high tragedies, and short and easy parts in genteel comedies, and jolly parts in farces - though I cannot tell why this was exactly; yet, now that I recall all the circumstances, I think I can see a little into the springs and motives which being cunningly presented to me under various disguises, induced me to set about performing the part I did, besides cajoling me into the delusion that it was a choice resulting from my own unbiased freewill and discriminating judgment.

Chief among these motives was the overwhelming idea of the great whale himself. Such a portentous and mysterious monster roused all my curiosity. Then the wild and distant seas where he rolled his island bulk; the undeliverable, nameless perils of the whale; these, with all the attending marvels of a thousand Patagonian sights and sounds, helped to sway me to my wish. With other men, perhaps, such things would not have been inducements; but as for me, I am tormented with an everlasting itch for things remote. I love to sail forbidden seas, and land on barbarous coasts. Not ignoring what is good, I am quick to perceive a horror, and could still be social with it - would they let me - since it is but well to be on friendly terms with all the inmates of the place one lodges in.

By reason of these things, then, the whaling voyage was welcome; the great flood-gates of the wonder-world swung open, and in the wild conceits that swayed me to my purpose, two and two there floated into my inmost soul, endless processions of the whale, and, mid most of them all, one grand hooded phantom, like a snow hill in the air.

Herman Melville - Moby Dick (1851)

Exercises

1. The main reason Ishmael is going down to the sea is:
   A. escape from depression
   B. relieve restlessness
   C. missing life aboard ship
   D. poverty
   E. the lure of travel

2. Ismael believes people are attracted to water because:
   A. the ocean promises adventure
   B. they need a change in routine
   C. all paths lead to water
   D. water makes for meditation
   E. so much of us is made of water

3. Ishmael sees water as a symbol of:
   A. power
   B. a mirror reflection
   C. solitude
   D. mystery
   E. divine creation

4. Going to sea as a passenger is said to be undesirable for all the following reasons except:
   A. passengers require entertaining
   B. passengers must pay
   C. passengers get seasick
   D. passengers may not sleep well
   E. passengers can get moody

5. Ishmael's vision of a snowhill refers to:
   A. a flock of gulls
   B. polar ice
   C. a cloud formation
   D. a mainsail
   E. a whale

6. Ishmael's occupation before going to sea was as a:
   A. preacher
   B. newspaperman
   C. accountant
   D. Latin translator
   E. teacher

7. Ishmael outlines a newspaper article featuring himself to indicate (lines 251-2):
   A. his essential insignificance
   B. the novelty of whaling
   C. his sense of adventure
   D. his desire for recognition
   E. the importance of his undertaking

8. The setting of the excerpt is:
   A. Nantucket
   B. New Bedford
   C. Gloucester
   D. Manhattan
   E. Providence

9. The negatives mentioned about his going to sea do not include:
   A. taking orders
   B. slave-like labor
   C. inherent danger
   D. reduction in status
   E. leaving land comrades behind

10. Ishmael's preferred rank in going to sea would be as a:
    A. simple sailor
    B. First mate
    C. Cook
    D. Captain
    E. Commodore

Harriet Beecher Stowe – Uncle Tom's Cabin (1852)

In Which the Reader Is Introduced to a Man of Humanity

Late in the afternoon of a chilly day in February, two gentlemen were sitting alone over their wine, in a well-furnished dining parlor, in the town of P----, in Kentucky. There were no servants present, and the gentlemen, with chairs closely approaching, seemed to be discussing some subject with great earnestness.

For convenience sake, we have said, hitherto, two gentlemen. One of the parties, however, when critically examined, did not seem, strictly speaking, to come under the species. He was a short, thick-set man, with coarse, commonplace features, and that swaggering air of pretension which marks a low man who is trying to elbow his way upward in the world. He was much over-dressed, in a gaudy vest of many colors, a blue neckerchief, bedropped gayly with yellow spots, and arranged with a flaunting tie, quite in keeping with the general air of the man. His hands, large and coarse, were plentifully bedecked with rings; and he wore a heavy gold watch-chain, with a bundle of seals of portentous size, and a great variety of colors, attached to it,--which, in the ardor of conversation, he was in the habit of flourishing and jingling with evident satisfaction.

His conversation was in free and easy defiance of Murray's Grammar, and was garnished at convenient intervals with various profane expressions, which not even the desire to be graphic in our account shall induce us to transcribe.

His companion, Mr. Shelby, had the appearance of a gentleman; and the arrrangements of the house, and the general air of the housekeeping, indicated easy, and even opulent circumstances. As we before stated, the two were in the midst of an earnest conversation.

"That is the way I should arrange the matter," said Mr. Shelby.

"I can't make trade that way--I positively can't, Mr. Shelby," said the other, holding up a glass of wine between his eye and the light.

"Why, the fact is, Haley, Tom is an uncommon fellow; he is certainly worth that sum anywhere,--steady, honest, capable, manages my whole farm like a clock."

"You mean honest, as niggers go," said Haley, helping himself to a glass of brandy.

"No; I mean, really, Tom is a good, steady, sensible, pious fellow. He got religion at a camp-meeting, four years ago; and I believe he really _did_ get it. I've trusted him, since then, with everything I have,--money, house, horses,--and let him come and go round the country; and I always found him true and square in everything."

"Some folks don't believe there is pious niggers Shelby," said Haley, with a candid flourish of his hand, "but I do. I had a fellow, now, in this yer last lot I took to Orleans--'t was as good as a meetin, now, really, to hear that critter pray; and he was quite gentle and quiet like. He fetched me a good sum, too, for I bought him cheap of a man that was 'bliged to sell out; so I realized six hundred on him. Yes, I consider religion a valeyable

thing in a nigger, when it's the genuine article, and no mistake."

"Well, Tom's got the real article, if ever a fellow had," rejoined the other. "Why, last fall, I let him go to Cincinnati alone, to do business for me, and bring home five hundred dollars. `Tom,' says I to him, `I trust you, because I think you're a Christian--I know you wouldn't cheat.' Tom comes back, sure enough; I knew he would. Some low fellows, they say, said to him--Tom, why don't you make tracks for Canada?' `Ah, master trusted me, and I couldn't,'--they told me about it. I am sorry to part with Tom, I must say. You ought to let him cover the whole balance of the debt; and you would, Haley, if you had any conscience."

"Well, I've got just as much conscience as any man in business can afford to keep,--just a little, you know, to swear by, as 't were," said the trader, jocularly; "and, then, I'm ready

to do anything in reason to 'blige friends; but this yer, you see, is a leetle too hard on a fellow--a leetle too hard." The trader sighed contemplatively, and poured out some more brandy.

"Well, then, Haley, how will you trade?" said Mr. Shelby, after an uneasy interval of silence.

"Well, haven't you a boy or gal that you could throw in with Tom?"

"Hum!--none that I could well spare; to tell the truth, it's only hard necessity makes me willing to sell at all. I don't like parting with any of my hands, that's a fact."

Here the door opened, and a small quadroon boy, between four and five years of age, entered the room. There was something in his appearance remarkably beautiful and engaging. His black hair, fine as floss silk, hung in glossy curls about his round, dimpled face, while a pair of large dark eyes, full of fire and softness, looked out from beneath the rich, long lashes, as he peered curiously into the apartment. A gay robe of scarlet and

yellow plaid, carefully made and neatly fitted, set off to advantage the dark and rich style of his beauty; and a certain comic air of assurance, blended with bashfulness, showed that he had been not unused to being petted and noticed by his master.

"Hulloa, Jim Crow!" said Mr. Shelby, whistling, and snapping a bunch of raisins towards him, "pick that up, now!"

The child scampered, with all his little strength, after the prize, while his master laughed.

"Come here, Jim Crow," said he. The child came up, and the master patted the curly head, and chucked him under the chin.

"Now, Jim, show this gentleman how you can dance and sing."

The boy commenced one of those wild, grotesque songs common among the negroes, in a rich, clear voice, accompanying his singing with many comic evolutions of the hands, feet, and whole body, all in perfect time to the music.

"Bravo!" said Haley, throwing him a quarter of an orange.

Exercises *Joel Chandler Harris - Brer Rabbit and the Tar-Baby (1880)*

1. Harley is characterized as all of the following <u>except</u>:
   A. snobbish
   B. vulgar
   C. showy
   D. foul-mouthed
   E. pretentious

2. The setting of this episode is:
   A. Kentucky
   B. Louisiana
   C. Mississippi
   D. Georgia
   E. Maryland

3. The main concern of Shelby and Haley's meeting is to discuss Tom's:
   A. trustworthiness
   B. religious piety
   C. honesty
   D. faithfulness
   E. sale

4. Haley says he has experienced a "nigger" who was:
   A. pious
   B. honest
   C. loyal
   D. not a flight risk
   E. profitable

5. Given the chance, Tom didn't escape because he'd therefore:
   A. feared capture and possible death
   B. be leaving his family behind
   C. be unChristian
   D. betray his master's trust
   E. be stealing from his master

6. In negotiating, Mr. Shelby appeals to Haley's:
   A. greed
   B. moral fairness
   C. business sense
   D. Christianity
   E. humanity

7. Mr. Shelby treats the quadroon boy as all the following except:
   A. a son
   B. an entertainment
   C. an object of laughter
   D. an object of affection
   E. an object of attention

8. From hints given, it's reasonable to assume the boy will probably soon:
   A. run off
   B. show affection for Mr. Shelby
   C. annoy Healy
   D. be part of the deal
   E. rush to his mother

9. Shelby's motive in selling Tom is:
   A. to complete a trade
   B. to pay a debt
   C. greed
   D. to keep a bargain
   E. to reduce his costs

10. The selection may be classified as:
    A. fantasy
    B. fable
    C. non-fiction
    D. documentary
    E. none of the above

Joel Chandler Harris - Brer Rabbit and the Tar-Baby (1880)

One evening recently, the lady whom Uncle Remus calls "Miss Sally" missed her little seven-year-old. Making search for him through the house and through the yard, she heard the sound of voices in the old man's cabin, and looking through the window, saw the child sitting by Uncle Remus. His head rested against the old man's arm, and he was gazing with an expression of the most intense interest into the rough, weather-beaten face that beamed so kindly upon him. This is what "Miss Sally" heard:

"Bimeby, one day, after Brer Fox bin doin' all dat he could fer ter ketch Brer Rabbit, en Brer Rabbit bin doin' all he could fer ter keep 'im fum it, Brer Fox say to hisse'f dat he'd put up a game on Brer Rabbit, en he ain't mo'n got de wuds out'n his mouf twel Brer Rabbit come a-lopin' up de big road, lookin' des ez plump en ez fat en ez sassy ez a Moggin hoss in a barley-patch.

"Hol' on dar, Brer Rabbit,' sez Brer Fox, sezee.

"I ain't got time, Brer Fox,' sez Brer Rabbit, sezee, sorter mendin' his licks.

"I wanter have some confab wid you, Brer Rabbit,' sez Brer Fox, sezee.

"All right, Brer Fox, but you better holler fum whar you stan': I'm monstus full er fleas dis mawnin',' sez Brer Rabbit, sezee.

"I seed Brer B'ar yistiddy,' sez Brer Fox, sezee, 'en he sorter raked me over de coals kaze you en me ain't make frens en live naberly, en I told him dat I'd see you.'

"Den Brer Rabbit scratch one year wid his off hine-foot sorter jub'usly, en den he ups en sez, sezee:

"All a-settin', Brer Fox. S'posen you drap roun' ter-morrer en take dinner wid me. We ain't got no great doin's at our house, but I speck de ole 'oman en de chilluns kin sort o' scramble roun' en git up sump'n fer ter stay yo' stummuck.'

"I'm 'gree'ble, Brer Rabbit,' sez Brer Fox, sezee.

"Den I'll 'pen on you,' says Brer Rabbit, sezee.

"Nex' day, Mr. Rabbit an' Miss Rabbit got up soon, 'fo day, en raided on a gyarden like Miss Sally's out dar, en got some cabbiges, en some roas'n-years, en some sparrer-grass, en dey fix up a smashin' dinner. Bimeby one er de little Rabbits, playin' out in de backyard, come runnin' in hollerin', 'Oh, ma! oh, ma! I seed Mr. Fox a-comin'!' En den Brer Rabbit he tuck de chilluns by der years en make um set down, and den him en Miss Rabbit sorter dally roun' waitin' for Brer Fox. En dey keep on waitin', but no Brer Fox ain't come. Atter while Brer Rabbit goes to de do', easy like, en peep out, en dar, stickin' out fum behime de cornder, wuz de tip-een' er Brer Fox's tail. Den Brer Rabbit shot de do' en sot down, en put his paws behime his years, en begin fer ter sing:

"De place wharbouts you spill de grease,
Right dar youer boun' ter slide,
An' whar you fine a bunch er ha'r,
You'll sholy fine de hide!'"

"Nex' day Brer Fox sont word by Mr. Mink en skuze hisse'f kaze he wuz too sick fer ter come, en he ax Brer Rabbit fer ter come en take dinner wid him, en Brer Rabbit say he wuz 'gree'ble.

"Bimeby, w'en de shadders wuz at der shortes', Brer Rabbit he sorter brush up en santer down ter Brer Fox's house, en w'en he got dar he yer somebody groanin', en he look in de do', en dar he see Brer Fox settin' up in a rockin'-cheer all wrop up wid flannil, en he look mighty weak. Brer Rabbit look all roun', he did, but he ain't see no dinner. De dish-pan wuz settin' on de table, en close by wuz a kyarvin-knife.

"Look like you gwineter have chicken fer dinner, Brer Fox,' sez Brer Rabbit, sezee.

"Yes, Brer Rabbit, deyer nice en fresh en tender,' sez Brer Fox, sezee.

"Den Brer Rabbit sorter pull his mustarsh, en say, 'You ain't got no' calamus-root, is you, Brer Fox? I done got so now dat I can't eat no' chicken 'ceppin' she's seasoned up wid calamus-root.' En wid dat Brer Rabbit lipt out er de do' and dodge 'mong de bushes, en sot dar watchin' fer Brer Fox; en he ain't watch long, nudder, kaze Brer Fox flung off de flannil en crope out er de house en got whar he could close in on Brer Rabbit, en bimeby Brer Rabbit holler out, 'Oh, Brer Fox! I'll des put yo' calamus-root out yer on dis yer stump. Better come git it while hit's fresh.' And wid dat Brer Rabbit gallop off home. En Brer Fox ain't never kotch 'im yit, en w'at's mo', honey, he ain't gwineter."

"Didn't the fox never catch the rabbit, Uncle Remus?" asked the little boy the next evening.

"He come mighty nigh it, honey, sho's you bawn—Brer Fox did. One day arter Brer Rabbit fool 'im wid dat calamus-root, Brer Fox went ter wuk en got 'im some tar, en mix it wid some turken-time, en fix up a contrapshun what he call a Tar-Baby, en he tuck dish yer Tar-Baby en he sot 'er in de big road, en den he lay off in de bushes fer ter see wat de news wuz gwineter be. En he didn't hatter wait long, nudder, kaze bimeby here come Brer Rabbit pacin' down de road—lippity-clippity, clippity-lippity—des ez sassy ez a jay-bird. Brer Fox he lay low. Brer Rabbit come prancin' 'long twel he spy de Tar-Baby, en den he fotch up on his behime legs like he was 'stonished. De Tar-Baby she sot dar, she did, en Brer Fox he lay low.

"Mawnin'!' sez Brer Rabbit, sezee; 'nice wedder dis mawnin',' sezee.

"Tar-Baby ain't sayin' nuthin' en Brer Fox he lay low.

"How duz yo' sym'tums seem ter segashuate?' sez Brer Rabbit, sezee.

"Brer Fox he wink his eye slow, en lay low, en de Tar-Baby she ain't sayin' nuthin'.

"How you come on, den? Is you deaf?' sez Brer Rabbit, sezee. 'Kaze if you is I kin holler louder,' sezee.

"Tar-Baby lay still, en Brer Fox he lay low.

"Youer stuck up, dat's w'at you is,' says Brer Rabbit, sezee, 'en I'm gwineter kyore you, dat's w'at I'm a-gwineter do,' sezee.

"Brer Fox he sorter chuckle in his stummuck, he did, but Tar-Baby ain't sayin' nuthin'.

"I'm gwineter larn you howter talk ter 'specttubble fokes ef hit's de las 'ack,' sez Brer Rabbit, sezee. 'Ef you don't take off dat hat en tell me howdy, I'm gwineter bus' you wide open,' sezee.

"Tar-Baby stay still, en Brer Fox he lay low.

"Brer Rabbit keep on axin' 'im, en de Tar-Baby she keep on sayin' nuthin', twel present'y Brer Rabbit draw back wid his fis', he did, en blip he tuck er side er de head. Right dar's whar he broke his merlasses-jug. His fis' stuck, en he can't pull loose. De tar hilt him. But Tar-Baby she stay still, en Brer Fox he lay low.

"Ef you don't lemme loose, I'll knock you ag'in,' sez Brer Rabbit, sezee; en wid dat he fotch 'er a wipe wid te udder han', en dat stuck. Tar-Baby she ain't sayin' nuthin', en Brer Fox he lay low.

"Tu'n me loose, of' I kick de natal stuffin' outen you,' sez Brer Rabbit, sezee; but de Tar-Baby she ain't sayin' nuthin'. She des hilt on, en den Brer Rabbit lose de use er his feet in de same way. Brer Fox he lay low. Den Brer Rabbit squall out dat ef de Tar-Baby don't tu'n 'im loose he butt 'er crank-sided. En den he butted, en his head got stuck. Den Brer Fox he santered fort', lookin' des ez innercent ez wunner yo' mammy's mockin'-birds.

"Howdy, Brer Rabbit?' sez Brer Fox, sezee. 'You look sorter stuck up dis mawnin',' sezee; en den he rolled on de groun', en laft en laft twel he couldn't laff no mo'. 'I speck you'll take dinner wid me dis time, Brer Rabbit. I done laid in some calamus-root, en I ain't gwineter take no skuse,' sez Brer Fox, sezee."

Here Uncle Remus paused, and drew a two-pound yam out of the ashes.

"Did the fox eat the rabbit?" asked the little boy to whom the story had been told.

"Dat's all de fur de tale goes," replied the old man. "He mout, en den ag'in he moutent. Some say Jedge B'ar come 'long en loosed 'im; some say he didn't. I hear Miss Sally callin'. You better run 'long."...

"Uncle Remus," said the little boy one evening, when he had found the old man with little or nothing to do, "did the fox kill and eat the rabbit when he caught him with the Tar-Baby?"

"Law, honey, ain't I tell you 'bout dat?" replied the old darky, chuckling slyly. "I 'clar ter grashus I ought er tole you dat; but ole man Nod wuz ridin' on my eyelids twel a leetle mo'n I'd 'a' dis'member'd my own name, en den on to dat here come yo' mammy hollerin' atter you.

"W'at I tell you w'en I fus' begin? I tole you Brer Rabbit wuz a monstus soon beas'; leas'ways dat's w'at I laid out fer ter tell you. Well, den, honey, don't you go en make no udder kalkalashuns, kaze in dem days Brer Rabbit en his family wuz at de head er de gang w'en enny racket wuz on han', en dar dey stayed. 'Fo' you begins fer ter wipe yo' eyes 'bout Brer Rabbit, you wait en see whar'bouts Brer Rabbit gwineter fetch up at. But dat's needer yer ner dar.

"W'en Brer Fox fine Brer Rabbit mixt up wid de Tar-Baby, he feel mighty good, en he roll on de groun' en laff. Bimeby he up 'n' say, sezee:

"Well, I speck I got you dis time, Brer Rabbit,' sezee; 'maybe I ain't but I speck I is. You been runnin' roun' here sassin' atter me a mighty long time, but I speck you done come ter de een' er de row. You bin cuttin' up yo' capers en bouncin' roun' in dis naberhood ontwel you come ter b'leeve yo'se'f de boss er de whole gang. En den youer allers some'rs whar you got no bizness,' sez Brer Fox, sezee. 'Who ax you fer ter come en strike up a 'quaintence wid dish yer Tar-Baby? En who stuck you up dar whar you iz? Nobody in de roun' worril. You des tuck en jam yo'se'f on dat Tar-Baby widout waitin' fer enny invite,' sez Brer Fox, sezee—' en dar you is, en dar you'll stay twel I fixes up a bresh-pile and fires her up, kaze I'm gwineter bobbycue you dis day, sho',' sez Brer Fox, sezee.

"Den Brer Rabbit talk mighty 'umble.

"I don't keer w'at you do wid me, Brer Fox,' sezee, 'so you don't fling me in dat brier-patch. Roas' me, Brer Fox,' sezee, 'but don't fling me in dat brier-patch,' sezee.

"Hit's so much trouble fer ter kindle a fier,' sez Brer Fox, sezee, 'dat I speck I'll hatter hang you,' sezee.

"Hang me des ez high ez you please, Brer Fox,' sez Brer Rabbit, sezee, 'but do fer de Lord's sake don't fling me in dat brier-patch,' sezee.

"I ain't got no string,' sez Brer Fox, sezee, 'en now I speck I'll hatter drown you,' sezee.

"Drown me ez deep ez you please, Brer Fox,' sez Brer Rabbit, sezee, 'but don't fling me in dat brier-patch,' sezee.

"Dey ain't no water nigh,' sez Brer Fox, sezee, 'en now I speck I'll hatter skin you,' sezee.

"Skin me, Brer Fox,' sez Brer Rabbit, sezee, 'snatch out my eyeballs, t'ar out my years by de roots, en cut off my legs,' sezee, 'but do please, Brer Fox, don't fling me in dat brier-patch,' sezee.

"Co'se Brer Fox wanter hurt Brer Rabbit bad ez he kin, so he cotch him by de behime legs en slung 'im right in de middle er de brier-patch. Dar wuz a considerbul flutter whar Brer Rabbit struck de bushes, en Brer Fox sorter hung roun' fer ter see what wuz gwineter happen. Bimeby he hear somebody call 'im, en way up de hill he see Brer Rabbit settin' cross-legged on a chinkapin log koamin' de pitch outen his har wid a chip. Den Brer Fox know dat he bin swop off mighty bad. Brer Rabbit wuz bleedzed fer ter fling back some er his sass, en he holler out:

"Bred en bawn in a brier-patch, Brer Fox; bred en bawn in a brier-patch!' en wid dat he skip out des ez lively ez a cricket in de embers."

Joel Chandler Harris - Brer Rabbit and the Tar-Baby (1880)

Exercises

1. Uncle Remus is not:
   A. elderly
   B. forgetful
   C. black
   D. the boy's uncle
   E. poor

2. The first time Uncle Remus interrupts the story midway is because:
   A. his yam is done cooking
   B. he's forgotten the ending
   C. he's run out of energy
   D. the boy is growing restless
   E. the boy's mother is looking for him

3. The word "brer" means:
   A. Master
   B. Briar
   C. Brother
   D. Bare-faced
   E. Brethren

4. Brer Rabbit is best characterized as:
   A. fearless
   B. trusting
   C. disrespectful
   D. clever
   E. gentlemanly

5. Brer Fox considers all the following stratagems against Brer Rabbit except:
   A. beating
   B. drowning
   C. skinning
   D. hanging
   E. burning

6. Brer Fox preparations for the dinner include:
   A. a carving knife
   B. a dish pan
   C. an invitation to Mr. Mink
   D. a flannel wrap
   E. a chicken

7. In the story, the Brer Rabbit tale is told by:
   A. Miss Sally
   B. Brer Rabbit
   C. Uncle Remus
   D. a seven year-old
   E. an unidentified narrator

8. The moral of this story is:
   A. take advantage of the home field
   B. sassiness is dangerous
   C. a temper can cause trouble
   D. nature is a survival struggle
   E. it has no moral

9. The language used by Uncle Remus is best described as:
   A. uneducated African
   B. slang
   C. black English
   D. a Southern dialect
   E. aboriginal

10. This story is best described as a:
    A. folk tale
    B. fable
    C. fairy tale
    D. allegory
    E. satire

AMBROSE BIERCE – AN OCCURRENCE AT OWL CREEK BRIDGE (1891)

A man stood upon a railroad bridge in northern Alabama, looking down into the swift water twenty feet below. The man's hands were behind his back, the wrists bound with a cord. A rope closely encircled his neck. It was attached to a stout cross-timber above his head and the slack fell to the level of his knees. Some loose boards laid upon the ties supporting the rails of the railway supplied a footing for him and his executioners--two private soldiers of the Federal army, directed by a sergeant who in civil life may have been a deputy sheriff. At a short remove upon the same temporary platform was an officer in the uniform of his rank, armed. He was a captain. A sentinel at each end of the bridge stood with his rifle in the position known as "support," that is to say, vertical in front of the left shoulder, the hammer resting on the forearm thrown straight across the chest--a formal and unnatural position, enforcing an erect carriage of the body. It did not appear to be the duty of these two men to know what was occurring at the center of the bridge; they merely blockaded the two ends of the foot planking that traversed it.

Beyond one of the sentinels nobody was in sight; the railroad ran straight away into a forest for a hundred yards, then, curving, was lost to view. Doubtless there was an outpost farther along. The other bank of the stream was open ground--a gentle slope topped with a stockade of vertical tree trunks, loop-holed for rifles, with a single embrasure through which protruded the muzzle of a brass cannon commanding the bridge. Midway up the slope between the bridge and fort were the spectators--a single company of infantry in line, at "parade rest," the butts of their rifles on the ground, the barrels inclining slightly backward against the right shoulder, the hands crossed upon the stock. A lieutenant stood at the right of the line, the point of his sword upon the ground, his left hand resting upon his right. Excepting the group of four at the center of the bridge, not a man moved. The company faced the bridge, staring stonily, motionless.

The sentinels, facing the banks of the stream, might have been statues to adorn the bridge. The captain stood with folded arms, silent, observing the work of his subordinates, but making no sign. Death is a dignitary who when he comes announced is to be received with formal manifestations of respect, even by those most familiar with him. In the code of military etiquette silence and fixity are forms of deference.

The man who was engaged in being hanged was apparently about thirty-five years of age. He was a civilian, if one might judge from his habit, which was that of a planter. His features were good—a straight nose, firm mouth, broad forehead, from which his long, dark hair was combed straight back, falling behind his ears to the collar of his well fitting frock coat. He wore a moustache and pointed beard, but no whiskers; his eyes were large and dark gray, and had a kindly expression which one would hardly have expected in one whose neck was in the hemp. Evidently this was no vulgar assassin. The liberal military code makes provision for hanging many kinds of persons, and gentlemen are not excluded.

The preparations being complete, the two private soldiers stepped aside and each drew away the plank upon which he had been standing. The sergeant turned to the captain, saluted and placed himself immediately behind that officer, who in turn moved apart one pace. These movements left the condemned man and the sergeant standing on the two ends of the same plank, which spanned three of the cross-ties of the bridge. The end upon which the civilian stood almost, but not quite, reached a fourth. This plank had been held in place by the weight of the captain; it was now held by that of the sergeant. At a signal from the former the latter would step aside, the plank would tilt and the condemned man go down between two ties. The arrangement commended itself to his judgement as simple and effective. His face had not been covered nor his eyes bandaged. He looked a moment at his "unsteadfast footing," then let his gaze wander to the swirling water of the stream racing madly beneath his feet. A piece of dancing driftwood caught his attention and his eyes followed it down the current. How slowly it appeared to move! What a sluggish stream!

He closed his eyes in order to fix his last thoughts upon his wife and children. The water, touched to gold by the early sun, the brooding mists under the banks at some distance down the stream, the fort, the soldiers, the piece of drift--all had distracted him. And now he became conscious of a new disturbance. Striking through the thought of his dear ones was sound which he could neither ignore nor understand, a sharp, distinct, metallic percussion like the stroke of a blacksmith's hammer upon the anvil; it had the same ringing quality. He wondered what it was, and whether immeasurably distant or near by-- it seemed both. Its recurrence was regular, but as slow as the tolling of a death knell. He awaited each new stroke with impatience and--he knew not why--apprehension. The intervals of silence grew progressively longer; the delays became maddening. With their greater infrequency the sounds increased in strength and sharpness. They hurt his ear like the trust of a knife; he feared he would shriek. What he heard was the ticking of his watch.

He unclosed his eyes and saw again the water below him. "If I could free my hands," he thought, "I might throw off the noose and spring into the stream. By diving I could evade the bullets and, swimming vigorously, reach the bank, take to the woods and get away home. My home, thank God, is as yet outside their lines; my wife and little ones are still beyond the invader's farthest advance."

As these thoughts, which have here to be set down in words, were flashed into the doomed man's brain rather than evolved from it the captain nodded to the sergeant. The sergeant stepped aside.

II

Peyton Farquhar was a well to do planter, of an old and highly respected Alabama family. Being a slave owner and like other slave owners a politician, he was naturally an original secessionist and ardently devoted to the Southern cause. Circumstances of an imperious nature, which it is unnecessary to relate here, had prevented him from taking service with that gallant army which had fought the disastrous campaigns ending with the fall of Corinth, and he chafed under the inglorious restraint, longing for the release of his energies, the larger life of the soldier, the opportunity for distinction. That opportunity, he felt, would come, as it comes to all in wartime.

Meanwhile he did what he could. No service was too humble for him to perform in the aid of the South, no adventure to perilous for him to undertake if consistent with the character of a civilian who was at heart a soldier, and who in good faith and without too much qualification assented to at least a part of the frankly villainous dictum that all is fair in love and war.

One evening while Farquhar and his wife were sitting on a rustic bench near the entrance to his grounds, a gray-clad soldier rode up to the gate and asked for a drink of water. Mrs. Farquhar was only too happy to serve him with her own white hands. While she was fetching the water her husband approached the dusty horseman and inquired eagerly for news from the front.

"The Yanks are repairing the railroads," said the man, "and are getting ready for another advance. They have reached the Owl Creek bridge, put it in order and built a stockade on the north bank. The commandant has issued an order, which is posted everywhere, declaring that any civilian caught interfering with the railroad, its bridges, tunnels, or trains will be summarily hanged. I saw the order."

"How far is it to the Owl Creek bridge?" Farquhar asked.

"About thirty miles."

"Is there no force on this side of the creek?"

"Only a picket post half a mile out, on the railroad, and a single sentinel at this end of the bridge."

"Suppose a man--a civilian and student of hanging--should elude the picket post and perhaps get the better of the sentinel," said Farquhar, smiling, "what could he accomplish?"

The soldier reflected. "I was there a month ago," he replied. "I observed that the flood of last winter had lodged a great quantity of driftwood against the wooden pier at this end of the bridge. It is now dry and would burn like tinder."

The lady had now brought the water, which the soldier drank. He thanked her ceremoniously, bowed to her husband and rode away. An hour later, after nightfall, he repassed the plantation, going northward in the direction from which he had come. He was a Federal scout.

III

As Peyton Farquhar fell straight downward through the bridge he lost consciousness and was as one already dead. From this state he was awakened--ages later, it seemed to him--by the pain of a sharp pressure upon his throat, followed by a sense of suffocation. Keen, poignant agonies seemed to shoot from his neck downward through every fiber of his body and limbs. These pains appeared to flash along well defined lines of ramification and to beat with an inconceivably rapid periodicity. They seemed like streams of pulsating fire heating him to an intolerable temperature. As to his head, he was conscious of nothing but a feeling of fullness--of congestion. These sensations were unaccompanied by thought. The intellectual part of his nature was already effaced; he had power only to feel, and feeling was torment. He was conscious of motion. Encompassed in a luminous cloud, of which he was now merely the fiery heart, without material substance, he swung through unthinkable arcs of oscillation, like a vast pendulum. Then all at once, with terrible suddenness, the light about him shot upward with the noise of a loud splash; a frightful roaring was in his ears, and all was cold and dark. The power of thought was restored; he knew that the rope had broken and he had fallen into the stream. There was no additional strangulation; the noose about his neck was already suffocating him and kept the water from his lungs. To die of hanging at the bottom of a river!--the idea seemed to him ludicrous. He opened his eyes in the darkness and saw above him a gleam of light, but how distant, how inaccessible! He was still sinking, for the light became fainter and fainter until it was a mere glimmer. Then it began to grow and brighten, and he knew that he was rising toward the surface--knew it with reluctance, for he was now very comfortable. "To be hanged and drowned," he thought, "that is not so bad; but I do not wish to be shot. No; I will not be shot; that is not fair."

He was not conscious of an effort, but a sharp pain in his wrist apprised him that he was trying to free his hands. He gave the struggle his attention, as an idler might observe the feat of a juggler, without interest in the outcome. What splendid effort!-- what magnificent, what superhuman strength! Ah, that was a fine endeavor! Bravo! The cord fell away; his arms parted and floated upward, the hands dimly seen on each side in the growing light. He watched them with a new interest as first one and then the other pounced upon the noose at his neck. They tore it away and thrust it fiercely aside, its undulations resembling those of a water snake. "Put it back, put it back!" He thought he shouted these words to his hands, for the undoing of the noose had been succeeded by the direst pang that he had yet experienced. His neck ached horribly; his brain was on fire, his heart, which had been fluttering faintly, gave a great leap, trying to force itself out at his mouth. His whole body was racked and wrenched with an insupportable anguish! But his disobedient hands gave no heed to the command. They beat the water vigorously with quick, downward strokes, forcing him to the surface. He felt his head emerge; his eyes were blinded by the sunlight; his chest expanded convulsively, and with a supreme and crowning agony his lungs engulfed a great draught of air, which instantly he expelled in a shriek!

He was now in full possession of his physical senses. They were, indeed, preternaturally keen and alert. Something in the awful disturbance of his organic system had so exalted and refined them that they made record of things never before perceived. He felt the ripples upon his face and heard their separate sounds as they struck. He looked at the forest on the bank of the stream, saw the individual trees, the leaves and the veining of each leaf--he saw the very insects upon them: the locusts, the brilliant bodied flies, the gray spiders stretching their webs from twig to twig. He noted the prismatic colors in all the dewdrops upon a million blades of grass.

The humming of the gnats that danced above the eddies of the stream, the beating of the dragon flies' wings, the strokes of the water spiders' legs, like oars which had lifted their boat--all these made audible music. A fish slid along beneath his eyes and he heard the rush of its body parting the water.

He had come to the surface facing down the stream; in a moment the visible world seemed to wheel slowly round, himself the pivotal point, and he saw the bridge, the fort, the soldiers upon the bridge, the captain, the sergeant, the two privates, his executioners. They were in silhouette against the blue sky. They shouted and gesticulated, pointing at him. The captain had drawn his pistol, but did not fire; the others were unarmed. Their movements were grotesque and horrible, their forms gigantic.

Suddenly he heard a sharp report and something struck the water smartly within a few inches of his head, spattering his face with spray. He heard a second report, and saw one of the sentinels with his rifle at his shoulder, a light cloud of blue smoke rising from the muzzle. The man in the water saw the eye of the man on the bridge gazing into his own through the sights of the rifle. He observed that it was a gray eye and remembered having read that gray eyes were keenest, and that all famous marksmen had them. Nevertheless, this one had missed.

A counter-swirl had caught Farquhar and turned him half round; he was again looking at the forest on the bank opposite the fort. The sound of a clear, high voice in a monotonous singsong now rang out behind him and came across the water with a distinctness that pierced and subdued all other sounds, even the beating of the ripples in his ears.

Although no soldier, he had frequented camps enough to know the dread significance of that deliberate, drawling, aspirated chant; the lieutenant on shore was taking a part in the morning's work. How coldly and pitilessly--with what an even, calm intonation, presaging, and enforcing tranquility in the men--with what accurately measured interval fell those cruel words:

"Company! . . . Attention! . . . Shoulder arms! . . . Ready!. . . Aim! . . . Fire!"

Farquhar dived--dived as deeply as he could. The water roared in his ears like the voice of Niagara, yet he heard the dull thunder of the volley and, rising again toward the surface, met shining bits of metal, singularly flattened, oscillating slowly downward. Some of them touched him on the face and hands, then fell away, continuing their descent. One lodged between his collar and neck; it was uncomfortably warm and he snatched it out.

As he rose to the surface, gasping for breath, he saw that he had been a long time under water; he was perceptibly farther downstream—nearer to safety. The soldiers had almost finished reloading; the metal ramrods flashed all at once in the sunshine as they were drawn from the barrels, turned in the air, and thrust into their sockets. The two sentinels fired again, independently and ineffectually.

The hunted man saw all this over his shoulder; he was now swimming vigorously with the current. His brain was as energetic as his arms and legs; he thought with the rapidity of lightning:

"The officer," he reasoned, "will not make that martinet's error a second time. It is as easy to dodge a volley as a single shot. He has probably already given the command to fire at will. God help me, I cannot dodge them all!"

An appalling splash within two yards of him was followed by a loud, rushing sound, DIMINUENDO, which seemed to travel back through the air to the fort and died in an explosion which stirred the very river to its deeps! A rising sheet of water curved over him, fell down upon him, blinded him, strangled him! The cannon had taken an hand in the game. As he shook his head free from the commotion of the smitten water he heard the deflected shot humming through the air ahead, and in an instant it was cracking and smashing the branches in the forest beyond.

"They will not do that again," he thought; "the next time they will use a charge of grape. I must keep my eye upon the gun; the smoke will apprise me--the report arrives too late; it lags behind the missile. That is a good gun."

Suddenly he felt himself whirled round and round--spinning like a top. The water, the banks, the forests, the now distant bridge, fort and men, all were commingled and blurred. Objects were represented by their colors only; circular horizontal streaks of color--that was all he saw. He had been caught in a vortex and was being whirled on with a velocity of advance and gyration that made him giddy and sick. In few moments he was flung upon the gravel at the foot of the left bank of the stream--the southern bank--and behind a projecting point which concealed him from his enemies. The sudden arrest of his motion, the abrasion of one of his hands on the gravel, restored him, and he wept with delight. He dug his fingers into the sand, threw it over himself in handfuls and audibly blessed it. It looked like diamonds, rubies, emeralds; he could think of nothing beautiful which it did not resemble. The trees upon the bank were giant garden plants; he noted a definite order in their arrangement, inhaled the fragrance of their blooms. A strange roseate light shone through the spaces among their trunks and the wind made in their branches the music of Aeolian harps. He had not wish to perfect his escape--he was content to remain in that enchanting spot until retaken.

A whiz and a rattle of grapeshot among the branches high above his head roused him from his dream. The baffled cannoneer had fired him a random farewell. He sprang to his feet, rushed up the sloping bank, and plunged into the forest.

All that day he traveled, laying his course by the rounding sun. The forest seemed interminable; nowhere did he discover a break in it, not even a woodman's road. He had not known that he lived in so wild a region. There was something uncanny in the revelation.

By nightfall he was fatigued, footsore, famished. The thought of his wife and children urged him on. At last he found a road which led him in what he knew to be the right direction. It was as wide and straight as a city street, yet it seemed untraveled. No fields

bordered it, no dwelling anywhere. Not so much as the barking of a dog suggested human habitation. The black bodies of the trees formed a straight wall on both sides, terminating on the horizon in a point, like a diagram in a lesson in perspective. Overhead, as he looked up through this rift in the wood, shone great golden stars looking

unfamiliar and grouped in strange constellations. He was sure they were arranged in some order which had a secret and malign significance. The wood on either side was full of singular noises, among which--once, twice, and again--he distinctly heard whispers in an unknown tongue.

His neck was in pain and lifting his hand to it found it horribly swollen. He knew that it had a circle of black where the rope had bruised it. His eyes felt congested; he could no longer close them. His tongue was swollen with thirst; he relieved its fever by thrusting

it forward from between his teeth into the cold air. How softly the turf had carpeted the untraveled avenue--he could no longer feel the roadway beneath his feet!

Doubtless, despite his suffering, he had fallen asleep while walking, for now he sees another scene--perhaps he has merely recovered from a delirium. He stands at the gate of his own home. All is as he left it, and all bright and beautiful in the morning sunshine. He must have traveled the entire night. As he pushes open the gate and passes up the wide white walk, he sees a flutter of female garments; his wife, looking fresh and cool and sweet, steps down from the veranda to meet him. At the bottom of the steps she stands waiting, with a smile of ineffable joy, an attitude of matchless grace and dignity. Ah, how beautiful she is! He springs forwards with extended arms. As he is about to clasp her he feels a stunning blow upon the back of the neck; a blinding white light blazes all about him with a sound like the shock of a cannon-- then all is darkness and silence!

Peyton Farquhar was dead; his body, with a broken neck, swung gently from side to side beneath the timbers of the Owl Creek bridge.

Ambrose Bierce – An Occurrence At Owl Creek Bridge (1891)

Exercises

1. The opening scene features all the following except: _____
   A. civilian spectators
   B. a stockade
   C. soldiers on a bridge
   D. a cannon
   E. a sentinel at each bridge end

2. The actual executioner is to be a:
   A. colonel
   B. lieutenant
   C. sergeant
   D. corporal
   E. private

3. The recurrent sound the condemned man hears is:
   A. a drumbeat
   B. rolling thunder
   C. his heartbeat
   D. a death knell
   E. a watch

4. Farquhar is all of the following except:
   A. a plantation owner
   B. a former soldier
   C. a family father
   D. a slave-holder
   E. a politician

5. The dusty horseman who visits Farquhar:
   A. is a Confederate spy
   B. is acting as a double agent
   C. encourages him to burn the bridge
   D. falsely describes bridge defenses
   E. leaves Farquhar after nightfall

6. Once falling into the river, Farquar is most fearful of:
   A. drowning
   B. not getting his hands untied
   C. being choked by the noose
   D. shots from soldiers on the bridge
   E. bullets of spectators on the bank

7. The striking feature of the story is its:
   A. photographic realism
   B. psychological realism
   C. romanticized nature description
   D. graphic portrayal of violence
   E. happy ending

8. The time between the beginning and end of the story is about:
   A. an afternoon and night
   B. a day
   C. an hour
   D. 15 minutes
   E. a moment

9. Farquhar seems to be:
   A. a Confederate agent
   B. a criminal
   C. a traitor
   D. a Southern sympathizer
   E. innocent

10. Farquhar is most afraid of:
    A. suffocation
    B. drowning
    C. hanging
    C. hanging and drowning
    E. being shot

KATE CHOPIN - THE STORY OF AN HOUR (1894)

Knowing that Mrs. Mallard was afflicted with a heart trouble, great care was taken to break to her as gently as possible the news of her husband's death.

It was her sister Josephine who told her, in broken sentences; veiled hints that revealed in half concealing. Her husband's friend Richards was there, too, near her. It was he who had been in the newspaper office when intelligence of the railroad disaster was received, with Brently Mallard's name leading the list of "killed." He had only taken the time to assure himself of its truth by a second telegram, and had hastened to forestall any less careful, less tender friend in bearing the sad message.

She did not hear the story as many women have heard the same, with a paralyzed inability to accept its significance. She wept at once, with sudden, wild abandonment, in her sister's arms. When the storm of grief had spent itself she went away to her room alone. She would have no one follow her.

There stood, facing the open window, a comfortable, roomy armchair. Into this she sank, pressed down by a physical exhaustion that haunted her body and seemed to reach into her soul.

She could see in the open square before her house the tops of trees that were all aquiver with the new spring life. The delicious breath of rain was in the air. In the street below a peddler was crying his wares. The notes of a distant song which some one was singing reached her faintly, and countless sparrows were twittering in the eaves.

There were patches of blue sky showing here and there through the clouds that had met and piled one above the other in the west facing her window.

She sat with her head thrown back upon the cushion of the chair, quite motionless, except when a sob came up into her throat and shook her, as a child who has cried itself to sleep continues to sob in its dreams.

She was young, with a fair, calm face, whose lines bespoke repression and even a certain strength. But now there was a dull stare in her eyes, whose gaze was fixed away off yonder on one of those patches of blue sky. It was not a glance of reflection, but rather indicated a suspension of intelligent thought.

There was something coming to her and she was waiting for it, fearfully. What was it? She did not know; it was too subtle and elusive to name. But she felt it, creeping out of the sky, reaching toward her through the sounds, the scents, the color that filled the air.

Now her bosom rose and fell tumultuously. She was beginning to recognize this thing that was approaching to possess her, and she was striving to beat it back with her will--as powerless as her two white slender hands would have been. When she abandoned herself a little whispered word escaped her slightly parted lips. She said it over and over under hte breath: "free, free, free!" The vacant stare and the look of terror that had followed it went from her eyes. They stayed keen and bright. Her pulses beat fast, and the coursing blood warmed and relaxed every inch of her body.

She did not stop to ask if it were or were not a monstrous joy that held her. A clear and exalted perception enabled her to dismiss the suggestion as trivial. She knew that she would weep again when she saw the kind, tender hands folded in death; the face that had never looked save with love upon her, fixed and gray and dead. But she saw beyond that bitter moment a long procession of years to come that would belong to her absolutely. And she opened and spread her arms out to them in welcome.

There would be no one to live for during those coming years; she would live for herself. There would be no powerful will bending hers in that blind persistence with which men and women believe they have a right to impose a private will upon a fellow-creature. A kind intention or a cruel intention made the act seem no less a crime as she looked upon it in that brief moment of illumination.

And yet she had loved him--sometimes. Often she had not. What did it matter! What could love, the unsolved mystery, count for in the face of this possession of self-assertion which she suddenly recognized as the strongest impulse of her being!

"Free! Body and soul free!" she kept whispering.

Josephine was kneeling before the closed door with her lips to the keyhold, imploring for admission. "Louise, open the door! I beg; open the door--you will make yourself ill. What are you doing, Louise? For heaven's sake open the door."

"Go away. I am not making myself ill." No; she was drinking in a very elixir of life through that open window.

Her fancy was running riot along those days ahead of her. Spring days, and summer days, and all sorts of days that would be her own. She breathed a quick prayer that life might be long. It was only yesterday she had thought with a shudder that life might be long.

She arose at length and opened the door to her sister's importunities. There was a feverish triumph in her eyes, and she carried herself unwittingly like a goddess of Victory. She clasped her sister's waist, and together they descended the stairs. Richards stood waiting for them at the bottom.

Some one was opening the front door with a latchkey. It was Brently Mallard who entered, a little travel-stained, composedly carrying his grip-sack and umbrella. He had been far from the scene of the accident, and did not even know there had been one. He stood amazed at Josephine's piercing cry; at

135 Richards' quick motion to screen him from the view of his wife.

When the doctors came they said she had died of heart disease--of the joy that kills.

Exercises

1. Josephine struggles to tell Mrs. Mallard of her husband's death because:
   A. she and Louise are not on good terms
   B. she doesn't like Brently Mallard
   C. Mrs. Mallard doesn't love her husband
   D. Mrs. Mallard has a heart condition
   E. the women are best friends

2. Mrs. Mallard's initial reactions to the news included all the following except:
   A. paralyzed silence
   B. wild weeping
   C. hugging her sister
   D. joy
   E. feeling liberated

3. Through her open window Mrs. Mallard perceives all the following except:
   A. a singer
   B. a peddler
   C. autumn leaves
   D. clouds
   E. birds

4. Before learning of her husband's death, Mrs. Mallard has feared:
   A. a long life
   B. being alone
   C. being free
   D. her husband's lack of love
   E. the shame of divorce

5. Josephine goes to the bedroom door fearing that her sister:
   A. may kill herself
   B. has fainted
   C. will become ill
   D. might be lonely
   E. might be delirious

6. Mrs. Mallory goes downstairs feeling:
   A. repressed
   B. beside herself
   C. proud
   D. victorious
   E. contented

7. Hearing his wife as he arrives, Brently thinks she is:
   A. hysterical
   B. indifferent
   C. shocked
   D. in pain
   E. overjoyed

8. In her room Mrs. Mallard imagines her husband:
   A. arriving home
   B. being asleep
   C. deserting her
   D. dead
   E. in old age

9. The doctors conclude that Mrs. Mallard died:
   A. in fear
   B. in pain
   C. in peace
   D. happy
   E. of shock

10. Mr. Mallard view of his wife is blocked by:
    A. his umbrella
    B. Josephine
    C. doctors
    D. Richards
    E. their children

Frank Baum - Wizard of Oz (1900)

The Cyclone

Dorothy lived in the midst of the great Kansas prairies, with Uncle Henry, who was a farmer, and Aunt Em, who was the farmer's wife. Their house was small, for the lumber to build it had to be carried by wagon many miles. There were four walls, a floor and a roof, which made one room; and this room contained a rusty looking cookstove, a cupboard for the dishes, a table, three or four chairs, and the beds. Uncle Henry and Aunt Em had a big bed in one corner, and Dorothy a little bed in another corner. There was no garret at all, and no cellar--except a small hole dug in the ground, called a cyclone cellar, where the family could go in case one of those great whirlwinds arose, mighty enough to crush any building in its path. It was reached by a trap door in the middle of the floor, from which a ladder led down into the small, dark hole.

When Dorothy stood in the doorway and looked around, she could see nothing but the great gray prairie on every side. Not a tree nor a house broke the broad sweep of flat country that reached to the edge of the sky in all directions. The sun had baked the plowed land into a gray mass, with little cracks running through it. Even the grass was not green, for the sun had burned the tops of the long blades until they were the same gray color to be seen everywhere. Once the house had been painted, but the sun blistered the paint and the rains washed it away, and now the house was as dull and gray as everything else.

When Aunt Em came there to live she was a young, pretty wife. The sun and wind had changed her, too. They had taken the sparkle from her eyes and left them a sober gray; they had taken the red from her cheeks and lips, and they were gray also. She was thin and gaunt, and never smiled now. When Dorothy, who was an orphan, first came to her, Aunt Em had been so startled by the child's laughter that she would scream and press her hand upon her heart whenever Dorothy's merry voice reached her ears; and she still looked at the little girl with wonder that she could find anything to laugh at.

Uncle Henry never laughed. He worked hard from morning till night and did not know what joy was. He was gray also, from his long beard to his rough boots, and he looked stern and solemn, and rarely spoke.

It was Toto that made Dorothy laugh, and saved her from growing as gray as her other surroundings. Toto was not gray; he was a little black dog, with long silky hair and small black eyes that twinkled merrily on either side of his funny, wee nose. Toto played all day long, and Dorothy played with him, and loved him dearly.

Today, however, they were not playing. Uncle Henry sat upon the doorstep and looked anxiously at the sky, which was even grayer than usual. Dorothy stood in the door with Toto in her arms, and looked at the sky too. Aunt Em was washing the dishes.

From the far north they heard a low wail of the wind, and Uncle Henry and Dorothy could see where the long grass bowed in waves before the coming storm. There now came a sharp whistling in the air from the south, and as they turned their eyes that way they saw ripples in the grass coming from that direction also.

Suddenly Uncle Henry stood up.

"There's a cyclone coming, Em," he called to his wife. "I'll go look after the stock." Then he ran toward the sheds where the cows and horses were kept.

Aunt Em dropped her work and came to the door. One glance told her of the danger close at hand.

"Quick, Dorothy!" she screamed. "Run for the cellar!"

Toto jumped out of Dorothy's arms and hid under the bed, and the girl started to get him. Aunt Em, badly frightened, threw open the trap door in the floor and climbed down the ladder into the small, dark hole. Dorothy caught Toto at last and started to follow her aunt. When she was halfway across the room there came a great shriek from the wind, and the house shook so hard that she lost her footing and sat down suddenly upon the floor.

Then a strange thing happened.

The house whirled around two or three times and rose slowly through the air. Dorothy felt as if she were going up in a balloon.

The north and south winds met where the house stood, and made it the exact center of the cyclone. In the middle of a cyclone the air is generally still, but the great pressure of the wind on every side of the house raised it up higher and higher, until it was at the very top of the cyclone; and there it remained and was carried miles and miles away as easily as you could carry a feather.

It was very dark, and the wind howled horribly around her, but Dorothy found she was riding quite easily. After the first few whirls around, and one other time when the house tipped badly, she felt as if she were being rocked gently, like a baby in a cradle.

Toto did not like it. He ran about the room, now here, now there, barking loudly; but Dorothy sat quite still on the floor and waited to see what would happen.

Once Toto got too near the open trap door, and fell in; and at first the little girl thought she had lost him. But soon she saw one of his ears sticking up through the hole, for the strong pressure of the air was keeping him up so that he could not fall. She crept to the hole, caught Toto by the ear, and dragged him into the room again, afterward closing the trap door so that no more accidents could happen.

Hour after hour passed away, and slowly Dorothy got over her fright; but she felt quite lonely, and the wind shrieked so loudly all about her that she nearly became deaf.
140 At first she had wondered if she would be dashed to pieces when the house fell again; but as the hours passed and nothing terrible happened, she stopped worrying and resolved to wait calmly and see what the future would bring.
145 At last she crawled over the swaying floor to her bed, and lay down upon it; and Toto followed and lay down beside her.

In spite of the swaying of the house and the
150 wailing of the wind, Dorothy soon closed her eyes and fell fast asleep.

Frank Baum - Wizard of Oz (1900)

Exercises

1. In line 14 it can be inferred from context that a "garret" is a/an:
   A. rope
   B. landing
   C. closet
   D. attic
   E. den

2. The land around the farmhouse is all the following except:
   A. flat
   B. treeless
   C. unpopulated
   D. drought-stricken
   E. unplowed

3. Aunt Em's reaction to Dorothy's laughter is:
   A. envious
   B. startled
   C. disbelieving
   D. angry
   E. amused

4. Uncle Henry is all of the following except:
   A. untalkative
   B. serious
   C. humorless
   D. panicky
   E. hard-working

5. One thing described as having a non-gray color is:
   A. the dog
   B. the house exterior
   C. Aunt Em's eyes
   D. the grass
   E. the front door

6. The cyclone cellar becomes the refuge taken by:
   A. Uncle Henry
   B. Toto
   C. Dorothy
   D. Aunt Em
   E. Toto, Dorothy, and Aunt EM

7. Dorothy and Toto end up:
   A. on the floor
   B. frightened
   C. injured
   D. worried
   E. in her bed

8. Aunt Em is initially startled when Dorothy arrives by the orphan's:
   A. clothing
   B. laughter
   C. screaming
   D. insecurity
   E. dog

9. When the cyclone tips the house, Dorothy begins to feel:
   A. panicky
   B. like in a cradle
   C. abandoned
   D. trapped
   E. dizzy

10. When the cyclone hits, Aunt Em:
    A. tries to rescue Uncle Henry
    B. tries to save Toto
    C. retreats through a trap door
    D. grabs Dorothy's hand
    E. is lifted up by the cyclone

JACK LONDON - CALL OF THE WILD (1903)

Into the Primitive

"Old longings nomadic leap,
Chafing at custom's chain;
Again from its brumal sleep
5 Wakens the ferine strain."

Buck did not read the newspapers, or he would have known that trouble was brewing, not alone for himself, but for every tide- water dog, strong of muscle and with
10 warm, long hair, from Puget Sound to San Diego. Because men, groping in the Arctic darkness, had found a yellow metal, and because steamship and transportation companies were booming the find, thousands of
15 men were rushing into the Northland. These men wanted dogs, and the dogs they wanted were heavy dogs, with strong muscles by which to toil, and furry coats to protect them from the frost.

20 Buck lived at a big house in the sun-kissed Santa Clara Valley. Judge Miller's place, it was called. It stood back from the road, half hidden among the trees, through which glimpses could be caught of the wide cool
25 veranda that ran around its four sides. The house was approached by gravelled driveways which wound about through wide-spreading lawns and under the interlacing boughs of tall poplars. At the rear things
30 were on even a more spacious scale than at the front. There were great stables, where a dozen grooms and boys held forth, rows of vine-clad servants' cottages, an endless and orderly array of outhouses, long grape ar-
35 bors, green pastures, orchards, and berry patches. Then there was the pumping plant for the artesian well, and the big cement tank where Judge Miller's boys took their morning plunge and kept cool in the hot af-
40 ternoon.

And over this great demesne Buck ruled. Here he was born, and here he had lived the four years of his life. It was true, there were other dogs. There could not but be other
45 dogs on so vast a place, but they did not count. They came and went, resided in the populous kennels, or lived obscurely in the

recesses of the house after the fashion of Toots, the Japanese pug, or Ysabel, the Mexican hairless,--strange creatures that rarely put nose out of doors or set foot to ground. On the other hand, there were the fox terriers, a score of them at least, who yelped fearful promises at Toots and Ysabel looking out of the windows at them and protected by a legion of housemaids armed with brooms and mops.

But Buck was neither house-dog nor kennel-dog. The whole realm was his. He plunged into the swimming tank or went hunting with the Judge's sons; he escorted Mollie and Alice, the Judge's daughters, on long twilight or early morning rambles; on wintry nights he lay at the Judge's feet before the roaring library fire; he carried the Judge's grandsons on his back, or rolled them in the grass, and guarded their footsteps through wild adventures down to the fountain in the stable yard, and even beyond, where the paddocks were, and the berry patches. Among the terriers he stalked imperiously, and Toots and Ysabel he utterly ignored, for he was king,--king over all creeping, crawling, flying things of Judge Miller's place, humans included.

His father, Elmo, a huge St. Bernard, had been the Judge's inseparable companion, and Buck bid fair to follow in the way of his father. He was not so large,--he weighed only one hundred and forty pounds,--for his mother, Shep, had been a Scotch shepherd dog. Nevertheless, one hundred and forty pounds, to which was added the dignity that comes of good living and universal respect, enabled him to carry himself in right royal fashion. During the four years since his puppyhood he had lived the life of a sated aristocrat; he had a fine pride in himself, was even a trifle egotistical, as country gentlemen sometimes become because of their insular situation. But he had saved himself by not becoming a mere pampered house-dog. Hunting and kindred outdoor delights had kept down the fat and hardened his muscles; and to him, as to the cold-tubbing races, the love of water had been a tonic and a health preserver.

And this was the manner of dog Buck was in the fall of 1897, when the Klondike strike dragged men from all the world into the frozen North. But Buck did not read the newspapers, and he did not know that Manuel, one of the gardener's helpers, was an undesirable acquaintance. Manuel had one besetting sin. He loved to play Chinese lottery. Also, in his gambling, he had one besetting weakness--faith in a system; and this made his damnation certain. For to play a system requires money, while the wages of a gardener's helper do not lap over the needs of a wife and numerous progeny.

The Judge was at a meeting of the Raisin Growers' Association, and the boys were busy organizing an athletic club, on the memorable night of Manuel's treachery. No one saw him and Buck go off through the orchard on what Buck imagined was merely a stroll. And with the exception of a solitary man, no one saw them arrive at the little flag station known as College Park. This man talked with Manuel, and money chinked between them.

"You might wrap up the goods before you deliver 'm," the stranger said gruffly, and Manuel doubled a piece of stout rope around Buck's neck under the collar.

"Twist it, an' you'll choke 'm plentee," said Manuel, and the stranger grunted a ready affirmative.

Buck had accepted the rope with quiet dignity. To be sure, it was an unwonted performance: but he had learned to trust in men he knew, and to give them credit for a wisdom that outreached his own. But when the ends of the rope were placed in the stranger's hands, he growled menacingly. He had merely intimated his displeasure, in his pride believing that to intimate was to command. But to his surprise the rope tightened around his neck, shutting off his breath. In quick rage he sprang at the man, who met him halfway, grappled him close by the throat, and with a deft twist threw him over on his back. Then the rope tightened mercilessly, while Buck struggled in a fury, his tongue lolling out of his mouth and his great chest panting futilely. Never in all his life had he been so vilely treated, and never in all his life had he been so angry. But his strength ebbed, his eyes glazed, and he knew nothing when the train was flagged and the two men threw him into the baggage car.

The next he knew, he was dimly aware that his tongue was hurting and that he was being jolted along in some kind of a conveyance. The hoarse shriek of a locomotive whistling a crossing told him where he was. He had traveled too often with the Judge not to know the sensation of riding in a baggage car. He opened his eyes, and into them came the unbridled anger of a kidnapped king. The man sprang for his throat, but Buck was too quick for him. His jaws closed on the hand, nor did they relax till his senses were choked out of him once more.

"Yep, has fits," the man said, hiding his mangled hand from the baggageman, who had been attracted by the sounds of struggle. "I'm takin' 'm up for the boss to 'Frisco. A crack dog-doctor there thinks that he can cure 'm."

Concerning that night's ride, the man spoke most eloquently for himself, in a little shed back of a saloon on the San Francisco water front.

Upton Sinclair - The Jungle (1906)

Exercises

1. Buck is from:
   A. the Yukon
   B. the Northland
   C. Puget Sound
   D. Santa Clara
   E. San Diego

2. Buck's original master is a:
   A. Lawyer
   B. Businessman
   C. Prospector
   D. Purebred dog breeder
   E. Raisin farmer

3. Buck is this breed of dog:
   A. mixed
   B. collie
   C. German shepherd
   D. Malamute
   E. Husky

4. Buck is described as a:
   A. house pet
   B. hunting dog
   C. guard dog
   D. playmate
   E. all of the above

5. The word "intimate" in line 137 means:
   A. threaten
   B. feign
   C. suggest
   D. declare
   E. simulate

6. Buck's reaction to Manuel is:
   A. unafraid
   B. loyal
   C. anxious
   D. affectionate
   E. aggressive

7. The stranger seems to be all of the following except:
   A. a gambler
   B. a prospector
   C. a brute
   D. a liar
   E. a braggart

8. The story takes during the days of the:
   A. Great Depression
   B. Gold Rush
   C. Old West
   D. Polar expeditions
   E. Chinese immigration

9. At the end of the passage, Buck is getting transported to:
   A. the Klondike
   B. Canada
   C. Alaska
   D. California
   E. Puget Sound

10. This story seems to be:
    A. history
    B. adventure
    C. sentimental
    D. a reminiscence
    E. a satire

UPTON SINCLAIR - THE JUNGLE (1906)

And shortly afterward one of these, a physician, made the discovery that the carcasses of steers which had been condemned as tubercular by the government inspectors, and which therefore contained ptomaines, which are deadly poisons, were left upon an open platform and carted away to be sold in the city; and so he insisted that these carasses be treated with an injection of kerosene--and was ordered to resign the same week! So indignant were the packers that they went farther, and compelled the mayor to abolish the whole bureau of inspection; so that since then there has not been even a pretense of any interference with the graft. There was said to be two thousand dollars a week hush money from the tubercular steers alone; and as much again from the hogs which had died of cholera on the trains, and which you might see any day being loaded into boxcars and hauled away to a place called Globe, in Indiana, where they made a fancy grade of lard.

Jurgis heard of these things little by little, in the gossip of those who were obliged to perpetrate them. It seemed as if every time you met a person from a new department, you heard of new swindles and new crimes. There was, for instance, a Lithuanian who was a cattle butcher for the plant where Marija had worked, which killed meat for canning only; and to hear this man describe the animals which came to his place would have been worthwhile for a Dante or a Zola. It seemed that they must have agencies all over the country, to hunt out old and crippled and diseased cattle to be canned. There were cattle which had been fed on "whisky-malt," the refuse of the breweries, and had become what the men called "steerly"-- which means covered with boils. It was a nasty job killing these, for when you plunged your knife into them they would burst and splash foul-smelling stuff into your face; and when a man's sleeves were smeared with blood, and his hands steeped in it, how was he ever to wipe his face, or to clear his eyes so that he could see? It was stuff such as this that made the "embalmed beef" that had killed several times as many United States soldiers as all the bullets of the Spaniards; only the army beef, besides, was not fresh canned, it was old stuff that had been lying for years in the cellars.

Then one Sunday evening, Jurgis sat puffing his pipe by the kitchen stove, and talking with an old fellow whom Jonas had introduced, and who worked in the canning rooms at Durham's; and so Jurgis learned a few things about the great and only Durham canned goods, which had become a national institution. They were regular alchemists at Durham's; they advertised a mushroom-catsup, and the men who made it did not know what a mushroom looked like. They advertised "potted chicken,"-- and it was like the boardinghouse soup of the comic papers, through which a chicken had walked with rubbers on. Perhaps they had a secret process for making chickens chemically--who knows? said Jurgis' friend; the things that went into the mixture were tripe, and the fat of pork, and beef suet, and hearts of beef, and finally the waste ends of veal, when they had any. They put these up in several grades, and sold them at several prices; but the contents of the cans all came out of the same hopper. And then there was "potted game" and "potted grouse," "potted ham," and "deviled ham"-- de-vyled, as the men called it. "De-vyled" ham was made out of the waste ends of smoked beef that were too small to be sliced by the machines; and also tripe, dyed with chemicals so that it would not show white; and trimmings of hams and corned beef; and potatoes, skins and all; and finally the hard cartilaginous gullets of beef, after the tongues had been cut out. All this ingenious mixture was ground up and flavored with spices to make it taste like something. Anybody who could invent a new imitation had been sure of a fortune from old Durham, said Jurgis' informant; but it was hard to think of anything new in a place where so many sharp wits had been at work for so long; where men welcomed tuberculosis in the cattle they were feeding, because it made them fatten more quickly; and where they bought up all the old rancid butter left over in the grocery stores of a continent, and "oxidized" it by a forced-air process, to take away the odor, rechurned it with skim milk, and sold it in bricks in the cities! Up to a year or two ago it had been the custom to kill horses in the yards--ostensibly for fertilizer; but after long agitation the newspapers had been able to make the public realize that the horses were being canned. Now it was against the law to kill horses in Packingtown, and the law was really complied with--for the present, at any rate. Any day, however, one might see sharp-horned and shaggy- haired creatures running with the sheep and yet what a job you would have to get the public to believe that a good part of what it buys for lamb and mutton is really goat's flesh!

There was another interesting set of statistics that a person might have gathered in Packingtown--those of the various afflictions of the workers. When Jurgis had first inspected the packing plants with Szedvilas, he had marveled while he listened to the tale of all the things that were made out of the carcasses of animals, and of all the lesser industries that were maintained there; now he found that each one of these lesser industries was a separate little inferno, in its way as horrible as the killing beds, the source and fountain of them all. The workers in each of them had their own peculiar diseases. And the wandering visitor might be skeptical about all the swindles, but he could not be skeptical about these, for the worker bore the evidence of them about on his own person-- generally he had only to hold out his hand.

There were the men in the pickle rooms, for instance, where old Antanas had gotten his death; scarce a one of these that had not some spot of horror on his person. Let a man so much as scrape his finger pushing a truck in the pickle rooms, and he might have a sore that would put him out of the world; all the joints in his fingers might be eaten by the acid, one by one. Of the butchers and floorsmen, the beef-boners and trimmers, and all those who used knives, you could scarcely find a person who had the use of his thumb; time and time again the base of it had been slashed, till it was a mere lump of flesh against which the man pressed the knife to hold it. The hands of these men would be criss- crossed with cuts, until you could no longer pretend to count them or to trace them. They would have no nails,--they had worn them off pulling hides; their knuckles were swollen so that their fingers spread out like a fan. There were men who worked in the cooking rooms, in the midst of steam and sickening odors, by artificial light; in these rooms the germs of tuberculosis might live for two years, but the supply was renewed every hour. There were the beef-luggers, who carried two-hundred-pound quarters into the refrigerator-cars; a fearful kind of work, that began at four o'clock in the morning, and that wore out the most powerful men in a few years. There were those who worked in the chilling rooms, and whose special disease was rheumatism; the time limit that a man could work in the chilling rooms was said to be five years. There were the wool-pluckers, whose hands went to pieces even sooner than the hands of the pickle men; for the pelts of the sheep had to be painted with acid to loosen the wool, and then the pluckers had to pull out this wool with their bare hands, till the acid had eaten their fingers off. There were those who made the tins for the canned meat; and their hands, too, were a maze of cuts, and each cut represented a chance for blood poisoning. Some worked at the stamping machines, and it was very seldom that one could work long there at the pace that was set, and not give out and forget himself and have a part of his hand chopped off. There were the "hoisters," as they were called, whose task it was to press the lever which lifted the dead cattle off the floor. They ran along upon a rafter, peering down through the damp and the steam; and as old Durham's architects had not built the killing room for the convenience of the hoisters, at every few feet they would have to stoop under a beam, say four feet above the one they ran on; which got them into the habit of stooping, so that in a few years they would be walking like chimpanzees. Worst of any, however, were the fertilizer men, and those who served in the cooking rooms. These people could not be shown to the visitor,-- for the odor of a fertilizer man would scare any ordinary visitor at a hundred yards, and as for the other men, who worked in tank rooms full of steam, and in some of which there were open vats near the level of the floor, their peculiar trouble was that they fell into the vats; and when they were fished out, there was never enough of them left to be worth exhibiting, -- sometimes they would be overlooked for days, till all but the bones of them had gone out to the world as Durham's Pure Leaf Lard!

Upton Sinclair - *The Jungle (1906)*

Exercises

1. All of the following are mentioned as complicit in the corruption except:
   A. Durham
   B. the press
   C. workers
   D. the mayor
   E. a doctor

2. The names of characters mentioned would seem to indicate they are:
   A. Asian
   B. Sicilian
   C. Irish
   D. Polish
   E. Hispanic

3. The war mentioned in which many soldiers died from eating foul meat was:
   A. Civil
   B. Panamanian
   C. Spanish-American
   D. Indian
   E. Philippine

4. The phrase "chicken with rubbers" in lines 69-70 is meant to suggest:
   A. irony
   B. protection
   C. filthy conditions
   D. toughness
   E. false advertising

5. Apparently, consumers of lamb are really eating meat made from:
   A. horses
   B. hogs
   C. goats
   D. beef organs
   E. chickens

6. One of the two "worst" factory jobs is said to be working as a:
   A. steam cook
   B. meat-cutter
   C. stamper
   D. carcass-hoister
   E. skinner

7. "The Jungle" is probably meant to evoke in the reader a sense of:
   A. confusion
   B. prejudice
   C. competitiveness
   D. nature
   E. the inhuman

8. One can correctly surmise that this book eventually led to the reforms in this Act:
   A. Civil Service
   B. Workmen's Compensation
   C. Pure Food and Drug
   D. Civil Rights
   E. Immigration

9. The tongues are logically cut out from the beef because they:
   A. can be dyed to mask mouth disease
   B. will not absorb chemicals
   C. will be used for sausage
   D. contain precious blood
   E. are edible

10. The hands of these workers are disfigured over time:
    A. pickle room workers
    B. beef boners
    C. floorsmen
    D. hide pullers
    E. all the above

O. Henry - Gift of the Magi (1906)

One dollar and eighty-seven cents. That was all. And sixty cents of it was in pennies. Pennies saved one and two at a time by bulldozing the grocer and the vegetable man and the butcher until one's cheeks burned with the silent imputation of parsimony that such close dealing implied. Three times Della counted it. One dollar and eighty-seven cents. And the next day would be Christmas.

There was clearly nothing to do but flop down on the shabby little couch and howl. So Della did it. Which instigates the moral reflection that life is made up of sobs, sniffles, and smiles, with sniffles predominating.

While the mistress of the home is gradually subsiding from the first stage to the second, take a look at the home. A furnished flat at $8 per week. It did not exactly beggar description, but it certainly had that word on the lookout for the mendicancy squad.

In the vestibule below was a letter-box into which no letter would go, and an electric button from which no mortal finger could coax a ring. Also appertaining thereunto was a card bearing the name "Mr. James Dillingham Young."

The "Dillingham" had been flung to the breeze during a former period of prosperity when its possessor was being paid $30 per week. Now, when the income was shrunk to $20, though, they were thinking seriously of contracting to a modest and unassuming D. But whenever Mr. James Dillingham Young came home and reached his flat above he was called "Jim" and greatly hugged by Mrs. James Dillingham Young, already introduced to you as Della. Which is all very good.

Della finished her cry and attended to her cheeks with the powder rag. She stood by the window and looked out dully at a gray cat walking a gray fence in a gray backyard. Tomorrow would be Christmas Day, and she had only $1.87 with which to buy Jim a present. She had been saving every penny she could for months, with this result. Twenty dollars a week doesn't go far. Expenses had been greater than she had calculated. They always are. Only $1.87 to buy a present for Jim. Her Jim. Many a happy hour she had spent planning for something nice for him. Something fine and rare and sterling--something just a little bit near to being worthy of the honor of being owned by Jim.

There was a pier-glass between the windows of the room. Perhaps you have seen a pier-glass in an $8 flat. A very thin and very agile person may, by observing his reflection in a rapid sequence of longitudinal strips, obtain a fairly accurate conception of his looks. Della, being slender, had mastered the art.

Suddenly she whirled from the window and stood before the glass. her eyes were shining brilliantly, but her face had lost its color within twenty seconds. Rapidly she pulled down her hair and let it fall to its full length.

Now, there were two possessions of the James Dillingham Youngs in which they both took a mighty pride. One was Jim's gold watch that had been his father's and his grandfather's. The other was Della's hair. Had the queen of Sheba lived in the flat across the airshaft, Della would have let her hair hang out the window some day to dry just to depreciate Her Majesty's jewels and gifts. Had King Solomon been the janitor, with all his treasures piled up in the basement, Jim would have pulled out his watch every time he passed, just to see him pluck at his beard from envy.

So now Della's beautiful hair fell about her rippling and shining like a cascade of brown waters. It reached below her knee and made itself almost a garment for her. And then she did it up again nervously and quickly. Once she faltered for a minute and stood still while a tear or two splashed on the worn red carpet.

On went her old brown jacket; on went her old brown hat. With a whirl of skirts and with the brilliant sparkle still in her eyes, she fluttered out the door and down the stairs to the street.

Where she stopped the sign read: "Mne. Sofronie. Hair Goods of All Kinds." One flight up Della ran, and collected herself, panting. Madame, large, too white, chilly, hardly looked the "Sofronie."

"Will you buy my hair?" asked Della.

"I buy hair," said Madame. "Take yer hat off and let's have a sight at the looks of it."

Down rippled the brown cascade.

"Twenty dollars," said Madame, lifting the mass with a practised hand.

"Give it to me quick," said Della.

Oh, and the next two hours tripped by on rosy wings. Forget the hashed metaphor. She was ransacking the stores for Jim's present.

She found it at last. It surely had been made for Jim and no one else. There was no other like it in any of the stores, and she had turned all of them inside out. It was a platinum fob chain simple and chaste in design, properly proclaiming its value by substance alone and not by meretricious ornamentation--as all good things should do. It was even worthy of The Watch. As soon as she saw it she knew that it must be Jim's. It was like him. Quietness and value--the description applied to both. Twenty-one dollars they took from her for it, and she hurried home with the 87 cents. With that chain on his watch Jim might be properly anxious about the time in any company. Grand as the watch was, he sometimes looked at it on the sly on account of the old leather strap that he used in place of a chain.

When Della reached home her intoxication gave way a little to prudence and reason. She got out her curling irons and lighted the gas and went to work repairing the ravages made by generosity added to love. Which is always a tremendous task, dear friends--a mammoth task.

Within forty minutes her head was covered with tiny, close-lying curls that made her look wonderfully like a truant schoolboy. She looked at her reflection in the mirror long, carefully, and critically.

"If Jim doesn't kill me," she said to herself, "before he takes a second look at me, he'll say I look like a Coney Island chorus girl. But what could I do--oh! what could I do with a dollar and eighty-seven cents?"

At 7 o'clock the coffee was made and the frying-pan was on the back of the stove hot and ready to cook the chops.

Jim was never late. Della doubled the fob chain in her hand and sat on the corner of the table near the door that he always entered. Then she heard his step on the stair away down on the first flight, and she turned white for just a moment. She had a habit for saying little silent prayer about the simplest everyday things, and now she whispered: "Please God, make him think I am still pretty."

The door opened and Jim stepped in and closed it. He looked thin and very serious. Poor fellow, he was only twenty-two--and to be burdened with a family! He needed a new overcoat and he was without gloves.

Jim stopped inside the door, as immovable as a setter at the scent of quail. His eyes were fixed upon Della, and there was an expression in them that she could not read, and it terrified her. It was not anger, nor surprise, nor disapproval, nor horror, nor any of the sentiments that she had been prepared for. He simply stared at her fixedly with that peculiar expression on his face.

Della wriggled off the table and went for him.

"Jim, darling," she cried, "don't look at me that way. I had my hair cut off and sold because I couldn't have lived through Christmas without giving you a present. It'll grow out again--you won't mind, will you? I just had to do it. My hair grows awfully fast. Say `Merry Christmas!' Jim, and let's be happy. You don't know what a nice-- what a beautiful, nice gift I've got for you."

"You've cut off your hair?" asked Jim, laboriously, as if he had not arrived at that patent fact yet even after the hardest mental labor.

"Cut it off and sold it," said Della. "Don't you like me just as well, anyhow? I'm me without my hair, ain't I?"

Jim looked about the room curiously.

"You say your hair is gone?" he said, with an air almost of idiocy.

"You needn't look for it," said Della. "It's sold, I tell you--sold and gone, too. It's Christmas Eve, boy. Be good to me, for it went for you. Maybe the hairs of my head were numbered," she went on with sudden serious sweetness, "but nobody could ever count my love for you. Shall I put the chops on, Jim?"

Out of his trance Jim seemed quickly to wake. He enfolded his Della. For ten seconds let us regard with discreet scrutiny some inconsequential object in the other direction. Eight dollars a week or a million a year--what is the difference? A mathematician or a wit would give you the wrong answer. The magi brought valuable gifts, but that was not among them. This dark assertion will be illuminated later on.

Jim drew a package from his overcoat pocket and threw it upon the table.

"Don't make any mistake, Dell," he said, "about me. I don't think there's anything in the way of a haircut or a shave or a shampoo that could make me like my girl any less. But if you'll unwrap that package you may see why you had me going a while at first."

White fingers and nimble tore at the string and paper. And then an ecstatic scream of joy; and then, alas! a quick feminine change to hysterical tears and wails, necessitating the immediate employment of all the comforting powers of the lord of the flat.

For there lay The Combs--the set of combs, side and back, that Della had worshipped long in a Broadway window. Beautiful combs, pure tortoise shell, with jewelled rims--just the shade to wear in the beautiful vanished hair. They were expensive combs, she knew, and her heart had simply craved and yearned over them without the least hope of possession. And now, they were hers, but the tresses that should have adorned the coveted adornments were gone.

But she hugged them to her bosom, and at length she was able to look up with dim eyes and a smile and say: "My hair grows so fast, Jim!"

And then Della leaped up like a little singed cat and cried, "Oh, oh!"

Jim had not yet seen his beautiful present. She held it out to him eagerly upon her open palm. The dull precious metal seemed to flash with a reflection of her bright and ardent spirit.

"Isn't it a dandy, Jim? I hunted all over town to find it. You'll have to look at the time a hundred times a day now. Give me your watch. I want to see how it looks on it."

Instead of obeying, Jim tumbled down on the couch and put his hands under the back of his head and smiled.

"Dell," said he, "let's put our Christmas presents away and keep 'em a while. They're too nice to use just at present. I sold the watch to get the money to buy your combs. And now suppose you put the chops on."

The magi, as you know, were wise men--wonderfully wise men--who brought gifts to the Babe in the manger. They invented the art of giving Christmas presents. Being wise, their gifts were no doubt wise ones, possibly bearing the privilege of exchange in case of duplication. And here I have lamely related to you the uneventful chronicle of two foolish children in a flat who most unwisely sacrificed for each other the greatest treasures of their house. But in a last word to the wise of these days let it be said that of all who give gifts these two were the wisest. O all who give and receive gifts, such as they are wisest. Everywhere they are wisest. They are the magi.

O. Henry - Gift of the Magi (1906)

Exercises

1. In the opening four paragraphs all the following are evidenced except:
   A. counting money
   B. Della's impoverished life
   C. holiday cheer
   D. a non-functional mailbox
   E. a non-working buzzer

2. The word "mendicancy" in line 22 can be deduced in context to mean:
   A. vice
   B. police
   C. furniture
   D. poverty
   E. home repair

3. The inclusion on the card of his middle name indicates Jim's:
   A. pride in his family name
   B. upper-class upbringing
   C. desire for higher status
   D. egotism
   E. vanity

4. Jim's reaction when he sees Della's changed appearance is:
   A. pleased
   B. angry
   C. amused
   D. embarrassed
   E. stunned

5. Jim is compared to a setter (line 170) to show he's:
   A. loyal
   B. affectionate
   C. upright
   D. motionless
   E. attentive

6. Della's initial reaction as she begins to open Jim's present is:
   A. alarm
   B. surprise
   C. joy
   D. tears
   E. laughter

7. Della cries out "Oh, oh!" as Jim opens his gift because she:
   A. is excited about her gift for Jim
   B. realizes she made a mistake
   C. realizes Jim made a mistake
   D. realizes they both made a mistake
   E. thinks Jim will be displeased

8. After disobeying his wife Jim smiles (line 263) because:
   A. their efforts are in vain
   B. he thinks the situation comic
   C. he knows their reciprocal error
   D. he feels stupid
   E. he wants to wait till next Christmas

9. Jim says "you had me going a while" (line 224) because:
   A. he had thought his was a perfect gift
   B. he thinks Della is displeased
   C. he's in on the joke
   D. he was tempted at first to leave
   E. he has rushed home

10. The author ultimately concludes the Magi are embodied by:
    A. gifts
    B. generosity
    C. poverty
    D. Della and Jim
    E. sacrifice

LANGSTON HUGHES - THANK YOU, M'AM (1958)

She was a large woman with a large purse that had everything in it but a hammer and nails. It had a long strap, and she carried it slung across her shoulder. It was about
5 eleven o'clock at night, dark, and she was walking alone, when a boy ran up behind her and tried to snatch her purse. The strap broke with the sudden single tug the boy gave it from behind. But the boy's weight
10 and the weight of the purse combined caused him to lose his balance. Instead of taking off full blast as he had hoped, the boy fell on his back on the sidewalk, and his legs flew up. The large woman simply
15 turned around and kicked him right square in his blue-jeaned sitter. Then she reached down, picked the boy up by his shirt front, and shook him until his teeth rattled.

After that the woman said, "Pick up my
20 pocketbook, boy, and give it here."

She still held him tightly. But she bent down enough to permit him to stoop and pick up her purse. Then she said, "Now ain't you ashamed of yourself?"

25 Firmly gripped by his shirt front, the boy said, "Yes'm."

The woman said, "What did you want to do it for?"

The boy said, "I didn't aim to."

30 She said, "You a lie!"

By that time two or three people passed, stopped, turned to look, and some stood watching.

"If I turn you loose, will you run?" asked
35 the woman.

"Yes'm," said the boy.

"Then I won't turn you loose," said the woman. She did not release him.

"Lady, I'm sorry," whispered the boy.

40 "Um-hum! And your face is dirty. I got a great mind to wash your face for you. Ain't you got nobody home to tell you to wash your face?"

"No'm," said the boy.

"Then it will get washed this evening," said the large woman, starting up the street, dragging the frightened boy behind her.

He looked as if he were fourteen or fifteen, frail and willow-wild, in tennis shoes and blue jeans.

The woman said, "You ought to be my son. I would teach you right from wrong. Least I can do right now is to wash your face. Are you hungry?"

"No'm," said the being dragged boy. "I just want you to turn me loose."

"Was I bothering *you* when I turned that corner?" asked the woman.

"No'm."

"But you put yourself in contact with me," said the woman. "If you think that that contact is not going to last awhile, you got another though coming. When I get through with you, sir, you are going to remember Mrs. Luella Bates Washington Jones."

Sweat popped out on the boy's face and he began to struggle. Mrs. Jones stopped, jerked him around in front of her, put a half nelson about his neck, and continued to drag him up the street. When she got to her door, she dragged the boy inside, down a hall, and into a large kitchenette-furnished room at the rear of the house. She switched on the light and left the door open. The boy could hear other roomers laughing and talking in the large house. Some of their doors were open, too, so he knew he and the woman were not alone. The woman still had him by the neck in the middle of her room.

She said, "What is your name?"

"Roger," answered the boy.

"Then, Roger, you go to that sink and wash your face," said the woman, whereupon she turned him loose — at last. Roger looked at the door — looked at the woman — looked at the door — and went to the sink.

"Let the water run until it gets warm," she said. "Here's a clean towel."

"You gonna take me to jail?" asked the boy, bending over the sink.

"Not with that face, I would not take you nowhere," said the woman. "Here I am trying to get home to cook me a bite to eat, and you snatch my pocketbook! Maybe, you ain't been to your supper either, late as it be. Have you?"

"There's nobody home at my house," said the boy.

"Then we'll eat," said the woman, "I believe you're hungry — or been hungry — to try to snatch my pocketbook."

"I want a pair of blue suede shoes," said the boy.

"Well, you didn't have to snatch my pocketbook to get some suede shoes," said Mrs. Luella Bates Washington Jones. "You could of asked me."

"M'am?"

The water dripping from his face, the boy looked at her. There was a long pause. A very long pause. After he had dried his face and not knowing what else to do, dried it again, the boy turned around, wondering what next. The door was open. He could make a dash for it down the hall. He could run, run, run, run, *run*!

The woman was sitting on the daybed. After a while she said, "I were young once and I wanted things I could not get."

There was another long pause. The boy's mouth opened. Then he frowned, but not knowing he frowned.

The woman said, "Um-hum! You thought I was going to say *but*, didn't you? You thought I was going to say, *but I didn't snatch people's pocketbooks*. Well, I wasn't going to say that." Pause. Silence. "I have done things, too, which

I would not tell you, son — neither tell God, if He didn't already know. So you set down while I fix us something to eat. You might run that comb through your hair so you will look presentable."

In another corner of the room behind a screen was a gas plate and an icebox. Mrs. Jones got up and went behind the screen. The woman did not watch the boy to see if he was going to run now, nor did she watch her purse, which she left behind her on the daybed. But the boy took care to sit on the far side of the room, away from the purse, where he thought she could easily see him out of the corner other eye if she wanted to. He did not trust the woman *not* to trust him. And he did not want to be mistrusted now.

"Do you need somebody to go to the store," asked the boy, "maybe to get some milk or something?"

"Don't believe I do," said the woman, "unless you just want sweet milk yourself. I was going to make cocoa out of this canned mild I got here."

"That will be fine," said the boy.

She heated some lima beans and ham she had in the icebox, made the cocoa, and set the table. The woman did not ask the boy anything about where he lived, or his folks, or anything else that would embarrass him. Instead, as they ate, she told him about her job in a hotel beauty shop that stayed open late, what the work was like, and how all kinds of women came in and out, blondes, red-heads, and Spanish. Then she cut him a half of her ten-cent cake.

"Eat some more, son," she said.

When they were finished eating she got up and said, "Now, here, take this ten dollars and buy yourself some blue suede shoes. And next time, do not make the mistake of latching onto *my* pocketbook *nor nobody else's*—because shoes got by devilish ways will burn your feet. I got to get my rest now. But from here on in, son,

I hope you will behave yourself."

She led him down the hall to the front door and opened it. "Goodnight! Behave yourself, boy!" she said, looking out into the street as he went down the steps.

The boy wanted to say something else other that "Thank you, m'am" to Mrs. Luella Bates Washington Jones, but although his lips moved, he couldn't even say that as he turned at the foot of the barren stoop and looked up at the large woman in the door. Then she shut the door.

Langston Hughes - Thank You, M'am (1958)

Exercises

1. The boy is caught stealing because of:
   A. the woman's strength
   B. a streetlight
   C. watchful neighbors
   D. falling down
   E. conscience

2. Both characters in the story are all of the following except:
   A. self-confident
   B. from poor families
   C. uneducated
   D. black
   E. urban

3. Roger wants money for:
   A. no real reason
   B. housing
   C. food
   D. his mother
   E. shoes

4. The woman says "you are going to to remember (me)", (line 64) meaning that at first she will:
   A. punish him squarely
   B. give him some money
   C. teach him some manners
   D. feed and respect him
   E. teach by example

5. The woman lets go of Roger so he can:
   A. run away if he wants
   B. stand on his own
   C. avoid further punishment
   D. wash up
   E. have some food

6. Once in Mrs. Jones' home, Roger doesn't run because:
   A. he doesn't want to disappoint her
   B. he wants to find more money to steal
   C. the big woman herself can stop him
   D. he realizes the woman is poor, too
   E. he can't get at the purse

7. The woman gives Roger a lesson in:
   A. self-confidence
   B. the value of money
   C. unselfishness
   D. good behavior
   E. racial pride

8. Mrs. Jones in the end gives Roger:
   A. her purse
   B. dinner
   C. a "good night"
   D. money
   E. a pair of shoes

9. Roger sits at the far side of the room (line 139) to:
   A. get distant from Mrs. Jones
   B. be near the door
   C. keep an eye on the purse
   D. show trustworthiness
   E. seem well behaved

10. When the boy leaves, he says:
    A. "See you again"
    B. "Thank you, M'am"
    C. "Next time"
    D. "I be mighty grateful"
    E. nothing

Answer Key

ANSWER KEY

On occasion an answer may vary if a student brings a new perspective to the story

World Literature

Adam-and-Eve
1. A 2. D 3. E 4. A 5. B
6. D 7. A 8. B 9. B 10. A

Homer-Odyssey
1. B 2. D 3. B 4. D 5. B
6. A 7. B 8. B 9. C 10. B

Cervantes-Don-Quixote
1. D 2. A 3. D 4. B 5. E
6. A 7. C 8. B 9. A 10. E

Grimm Brothers -- Cinderella
1. D 2. E 3. E 4. D 5. A
6. D 7. D 8. D 9. E 10. D

Anton Chekhov -A Slander
1. E 2. C 3. C 4. E 5. D
6. A 7. B 8. C 9. A 10. C

Answer Key

English Literature

Sir Thomas Malory -- Morte-D'Arthur
1. A   2. E   3. B   4. D   5. A
6. D   7. C   8. D   9. A   10. A

Shakespeare – Henry V
1. A   2. D   3. D   4. D   5. E
6. A   7. D   8. E   9. A   10. A

Jonathan Swift -- Gullivers-Travels
1. C   2. E   3. A   4. B   5. B
6. D   7. C   8. D   9. B   10. E

Charles Dickens – A Tale of Two Cities
1. A   2. B   3. E   4. C   5. D
6. A   7. B   8. A   9. D   10. E

Lewis Carroll –Through the Looking-Glass
1. C   2. A   3. D   4. D   5. D
6. A   7. E   8. A   9. C   10. A

H.G. Wells – The Time Machine
1. D   2. E   3. A   4. E   5. B
6. D   7. E   8. A   9. D   10. C

Rudiard Kipling – How the Leopard Got His-Spots
1. C   2. E   3. D   4. C   5. D
6. C   7. A   8. C   9. D   10. D

Kenneth Grahame -- Wind-in-the-Willows
1. D   2. A   3. C   4. B   5. E
6. D   7. B   8. E   9. A   10. C

Saki – The Interlopers
1. A   2. E   3. D   4. A   5. E
6. A   7. D   8. E   9. E   10. A

Answer Key

American Literature

Edgar-Allen-Poe – The Tell-Tale Heart

| 1. E | 2. C | 3. C | 4. C | 5. D |
| 6. E | 7. A | 8. D | 9. A | 10. D |

Herman Melville -- Moby-Dick

| 1. A | 2. C | 3. D | 4. A | 5. E |
| 6. E | 7. A | 8. D | 9. E | 10. A |

Harriet Beecher Stowe – Uncle Tom's Cabin

| 1. A | 2. A | 3. E | 4. A | 5. D |
| 6. C | 7. A | 8. D | 9. B | 10. E |

Joel Chandlet Harris -- Brer-Rabbit

| 1. D | 2. E | 3. C | 4. D | 5. A |
| 6. B | 7. C | 8. E | 9. D | 10. A |

Ambrose Bierce -- Owl-Creek-Bridge

| 1. A | 2. C | 3. E | 4. B | 5. D |
| 6. D | 7. B | 8. E | 9. A | 10. E |

Kate Chopin – The Story Of An Hour

| 1. D | 2. D | 3. C | 4. C | 5. C |
| 6. D | 7. A | 8. D | 9. D | 10. D |

Frank Baum -- Wizard-of-Oz

| 1. D | 2. E | 3. B | 4. D | 5. A |
| 6. D | 7. E | 8. B | 9. B | 10. C |

Jack London -- Call-of-the-Wild

| 1. D | 2. E | 3. A | 4. E | 5. C |
| 6. A | 7. B | 8. C | 9. D | 10. B |

Upton Sinclair – The Jungle

| 1. B | 2. D | 3. C | 4. E | 5. C |
| 6. A | 7. E | 8. C | 9. E | 10. E |

O'Henry – Gift of the Magi

| 1. C | 2. D | 3. E | 4. E | 5. D |
| 6. C | 7. A | 8. B | 9. A | 10. D |

Langston Hughes – Thank You, Ma'm

| 1. D | 2. A | 3. E | 4. C | 5. D |
| 6. A | 7. D | 8. D | 9. D | 10. E |

www.ingramcontent.com/pod-product-compliance
Lightning Source LLC
Chambersburg PA
CBHW082044250426
43661CB00080B/2777